STRUCTURALISM AND
POSTSTRUCTURALISM

FOR BEGINNERS™

DONALD D. PALMER

For Beginners LLC
62 East Starrs Plain Road
Danbury, CT 06810 USA
www.forbeginnersbooks.com

A For Beginners® Documentary Comic Book
Originally published by Writers and Readers, Inc.
Copyright © 1997

Cataloging-in-publication information is available from the Library of Congress.

ISBN-10 # 1-934389-10-2 Trade
ISBN-13 # 978-1-934389-10-2 Trade

Manufactured in the United States of America

For Beginners® and Beginners Documentary Comic Books® are published by For Beginners LLC.

Reprint Edition

STRUCTURALISM AND POSTSTRUCTURALISM

FOR BEGINNERS™

Contents

The subject is spoken rather than speaking.

To Leila

What is Structuralism?
How is it possible?

And once the <u>structures</u> of structuralism have been discovered,

how is
Post-Structuralism
possible?

In its less dramatic versions, structuralism is just a <u>method</u> of studying language, society, and the works of artists and novelists. But in its most exuberant form, it is a philosophy, a <u>Weltanschauung</u>, an overall worldview that provides an **ORGANIC** as opposed to an **ATOMISTIC** account of reality and knowledge.

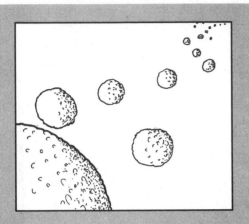 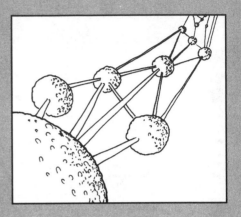

An atomistic view of the world sees reality as composed of discrete, irreducible units. The <u>parts</u> ("atoms") are more real than the <u>whole</u>.

An organic view of the world sees reality as a TOTALITY, as an organism. The parts are real only insofar as they are related to each other and to the whole.

According to the most radical version of structuralist organicism, reality is composed not of "THINGS," but of RELATIONSHIPS.

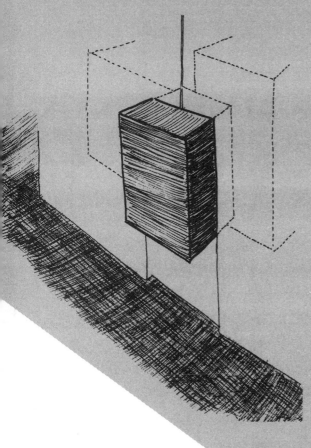

When structuralists and "post-structuralists" make the apparently outrageous claim that every "object" is both a <u>presence</u> and an <u>absence</u>, they mean that an object is never fully "There"— it is there to the extent that it appears before us, but it is Not there insofar as its being is determined by its relation to the whole system of which it is a part, a system that does not appear to us. In this sense, each "object," even in its quasi-absence, reflects the total system, and the total system is present in each of its parts.

Because structuralism claims to discover <u>permanent structures</u> behind or beneath things, its analyses tend to be SYNCHRONIC (ahistorical) rather than DIACHRONIC (historical). Its most extreme practitioners deny the significance of history, or are nostalgic for primitive cultures that are oblivious to the existence of change, cultures that are themselves ahistorical.

THAT'S ODD. IT LOOKS JUST LIKE A FRENCH ANTHROPOLOGIST.

THE UNCHANGING SPHINX, INDIFFERENT TO THE SANDS OF TIME

Because structuralism is concerned with a universal, unchanging order of things (what one of its members, Jacques Lacan, called the "Symbolic Order"), it is in many respects opposed to the "existentialism" of Jean-Paul Sartre that preceded it on the intellectual scene in Europe, or to any other form of humanism that emphasizes the individual.

I SAY, EXISTENCE PRECEDES ESSENCE

AND I SAY THERE IS ONLY ESSENCE

NOOOooo...

THE DISAPPEARANCE OF THE SUBJECT

In structuralism, there is a "disappearance of the subject," as she is spawned by, and absorbed back into, the general structure.

Because of these features, structuralism can claim as its ancestors the classical Continental rationalist philosophers of the seventeenth century rather than the British empiricists who are the creators of the Anglo-American intellectual environment.

LOCKE   BERKELEY   HUME

The empiricists (John Locke, George Berkeley, David Hume) believed that knowledge of the world was <u>IMMEDIATE</u>. The mind is a blank slate at birth, and reality impresses itself upon that slate in the form of the data of the five senses. These sense-data are "the given." They are the building blocks of our knowledge of the world. (Sense-data are the "atoms" of the empiricists' atomism.)

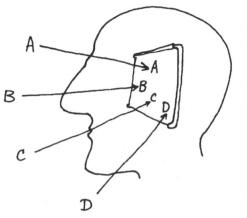

DESCARTES   SPINOZA   LEIBNIZ   KANT

On the contrary, the rationalists (René Descartes, Baruch Spinoza, Gottfried Leibniz, Immanual Kant), taking a cue from Plato, claimed that knowledge of the world is <u>MEDIATE</u>. It is mediated by innate ideas or innate structures (ideas or categories that are present at birth.) By attending to these innate components, we can deduce the universal structure of reality, a structure that will contradict the mere appearances provided by the senses and show itself to be a UNIVERSAL, unchanging truth, one best articulated in terms of mathematical formulas.

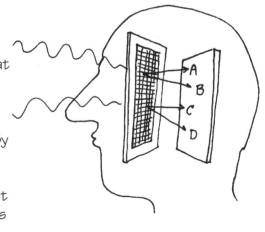

Ever since the seventeenth century, British and American thinkers have almost always been more influenced by the EMPIRICIST philosophers, and Continental European thinkers have been more influenced by the RATIONALIST philosophers.

Two modern examples of such Continental thinkers (and ones who have had a direct impact on structuralism) are KARL MARX (1818-1886) and SIGMUND FREUD (1856-1939). Both of these men thought of themselves as scientists, hence as "empiricists" in some sense, but they were clearly much more influenced by the rationalist philosophers than by the empiricist philosophers.

SOCIAL REALITY IS NOT CAUSED BY THE PROJECTS OF CONSCIOUSNESS, AND THE TRUTH ABOUT SOCIAL REALITY IS NOT GRASPED BY IMMEDIATE CONSCIOUSNESS

According to Marx,

There is, according to Marx, AN UNDERLYING STRUCTURE THAT DETERMINES SOCIAL REALITY, AND THAT MUST BE GRASPED IF SOCIAL REALITY IS TO BE UNDERSTOOD. For him, this <u>underlying structure</u> was an <u>economic</u> <u>one</u>. Its foundation is:

NATURAL RESOURCES

MEANS OF PRODUCTION

MEANS OF DISTRIBUTION

KARL'S LUMBER & HARDWARE OUTLET

CULTURAL FACTS	
LEGAL & POLITICAL FACTS	⌐ SUPERSTRUCTUR
SOCIO-ECONOMIC FACTS	— FOUNDATION

This underlying structure is tantamount to the "sum total" of all the RELATIONS OF PRODUCTION. Furthermore, everything else in society must be understood as being built upon that foundation. This "super-structure" is a "reflex" or a "sublimate" of that underlying structure.

It is essentially an ideo-logical reflection of the forces at work in the socio-economic founda-tion. For example, a POLITICAL CONSTITUTION is just a legalizing of the privileges of the social class that owns the eco-nomic foundation of the society.

THE GOVERNMENT SHALL NOT INTER-FERE IN THE PURSUIT OF FREE ENTERPRISE EXCEPT WHERE THE PUBLIC GOOD IS OTHERWISE AT RISK.

SHALL WE FEED THE SLAVES NOW?

SHHH. I'M PHILOSOPHIZING

CELEBRATE PRIVATE PROPERTY WEEK

The police are just heavily armed hired thugs who enforce the "rights" of the owning class. So-called morality is also the ideological defense of these advantages. The same with most art, liter-ature, poetry, religious preaching, and what passes for science.

8

They are all **CAPTIVES OF A PRIMARY STRUCTURE,** but are unable to understand themselves as anything but free.

Like structuralism, Marxism is a form of organicism and is anti-individualistic. Nevertheless, despite being <u>almost</u> a form of structuralism, ultimately Marxism is <u>not</u>, because of its obsession with HISTORY. Structualism is a SYNCHRONIC science, hence it is ahistorical. Nevertheless, Marxism deeply influenced structuralism, and a famous French Marxist, Louis Althusser, tried to synthesize his Marxism with structuralist arguments.

SIGMUND FREUD's <u>psychoanalysis</u> also has some important similarities with structuralism, and strongly influenced it. In psychoanalysis, too, what appears in consciousness is often very different from the truth which those "appearances" mask— a truth that can only be derived from the study of the STRUCTURAL ORGANIZATION OF THE UNCONSCIOUS MIND.

This underlying structure of which the conscious mind is unaware produces a tension between natural animal forces with the forces of civilization (i.e., basic sexual and aggressive instincts aligned against the interests of society that try to repress those instincts).

According to psychoanalytic theory there are three agencies at work in this dynamic: THE ID (an irrational, violent rapacious force demanding immediate gratification of its need for total pleasure), THE SUPEREGO (an irrational counterforce organized to control the demands of the id through the use of guilt), and THE EGO (composed of a rational, socially oriented conscious mind, and an unconscious CENSORING DEVICE that keeps much of the information about the battle between the id and the superego out of consciousness).

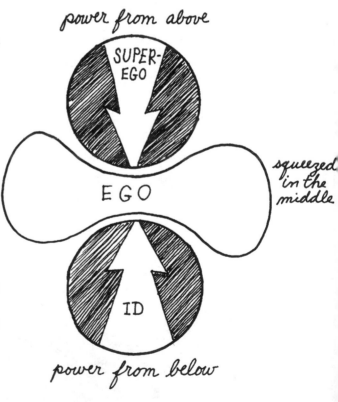

power from above

SUPER-EGO

EGO

squeezed in the middle

ID

power from below

The main function of the ego is that of <u>compromise</u> between id and superego, through delaying tactics ("There's a time and a place for everything"), or through displacement and sublimation.

Despite this "structural" analysis of the mind, ultimately traditional psychoanalysis is incompatible with structuralism because, like Marxism, it is DIACHRONIC. It is oriented toward history. For Freud, these structures can only be understood by tracing them back historically, to the infancy or childhood of the individual ("ONTOGENY"), or to the infancy or childhood of the human race ("PHYLOGENY"), where, according to Freud, the whole mess (that is, human culture and the human mind) began with the PRIMORDIAL PATRICIDE— an act of father murder and father cannibalism.

Still, psychoanalysis has deeply influenced both structuralism and post-structuralism, and we will see that Jacques Lacan, who has been called both names, tries to synthesize psycho-analysis with structuralist principles.

Furthermore, what both Marx and Freud lack is the mark that all structuralists and post-structuralists have in common despite the many, many differences among them, namely, a <u>lexicon</u>, that is, a technical vocabulary that derives from the Swiss linguist,

FERDINAND DE SAUSSURE

(1857-1913),

(the pronunciation is somewhere between "Sa sue ér" and "So see ér"),

who influenced every aspect of the movement, even though the term "structuralism" postdates Saussure by fifty years. It is to his work that we must now turn.

Saussure was born in Geneva into a family that had produced several noteworthy natural scientists. He too studied science but had a passion for languages. By the time he was fifteen he knew French, German, English, Latin, and Greek. He began his studies at the University of Geneva and continued them at the Universities of Berlin and Leipzig, where he earned his doctorate at the age of twenty-three. After teaching some time in Paris, he returned to his hometown of Geneva as a full professor having received a knighthood in the French Legion of Honor. He had published his first book when he was only twenty-one, but he found it more and more difficult to write after that. Between 1907 and 1911 he presented a series of lectures that, after his death at fifty-six, were reconstructed through his notes and those of his students and were published as A Course in General Linguistics, a book that was to thrust the young science of linguistics into prominence and one that would prove to be highly influential when its ideas were incorporated into structuralism some fifty years later.

We can examine Saussure's revolutionary importance by comparing and contrasting his view of the linguistic tradition inaugurated in ancient Greece by PLATO (427-347 BC), who argued that words do not name <u>things</u> in the world. (They <u>couldn't</u> do that, because there are too <u>many</u> things in the world, and they are all different from each other. If words named <u>things</u>, there would have to be as many names as there are things.)

Rather, according to Plato, words name CONCEPTS, IDEAS, which themselves are abstractions, designating ESSENCES, namely, that which a number of individuals have in common by virtue of which they are identifiable. (There can be many different kinds of triangles —acute, right, isosceles,— but the word "TRIANGLE" denotes what <u>all</u> triangles have in common, namely, three sides and three angles; that is, it designates the triangle's TRIANGULARITY. Similarly, the word "DOG" must denote what all dogs have in common, namely, DOGNESS.)

FAKE!

These essences, by the way, are not <u>merely</u> abstractions for Plato. They are <u>real</u>— in fact, more real than are the many physical manifestations of them that exist on earth, which are nothing but mere copies of the real thing, which exists in a Platonic heaven of Ideas as an eternal, unchanging truth.

WE <u>CALL</u> THEM DOGS BECAUSE THEY <u>ARE</u> DOGS

Furthermore, for Plato, there is some natural connection between words and concepts. Just as the word "writing" is like the idea of writing, so is the word "dog" somehow like the idea of a dog.

Well, what about Saussure? How much of this does he agree with?

NOT A HECK OF A LOT!

He <u>does</u> agree with one important point, however. Words name <u>ideas</u>, not things. There the similarities between Saussure and Plato end. What defines a word for Saussure is not its relation to some eternal essence; rather, what defines it is the relation in which it stands to <u>other</u> words in the system. Furthermore, these relations are NEGATIVE, not positive.

IN LANGUAGE THERE ARE ONLY DIFFERENCES <u>WITHOUT</u> <u>POSITIVE</u> <u>TERMS.</u>

THE IMPORTANT THING IN THE WORD IS NOT THE SOUND ALONE BUT THE PHONIC DIFFERENCES THAT MAKE IT POSSIBLE TO DISTINGUISH THIS WORD FROM ALL OTHERS.

Take the consonants "B" and "T." Place between them all the possible vowels in English.

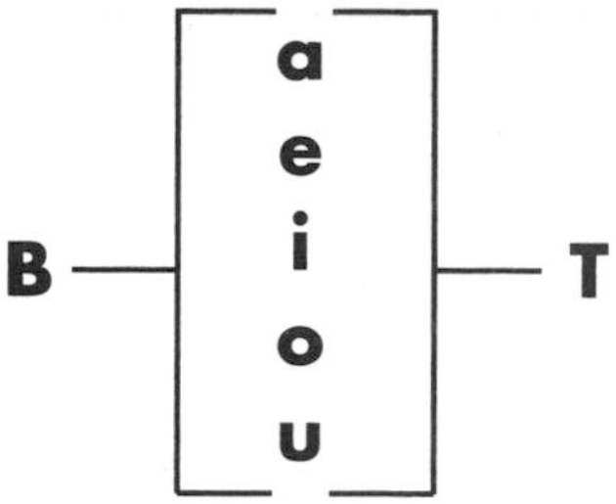

B — [a e i o u] — T

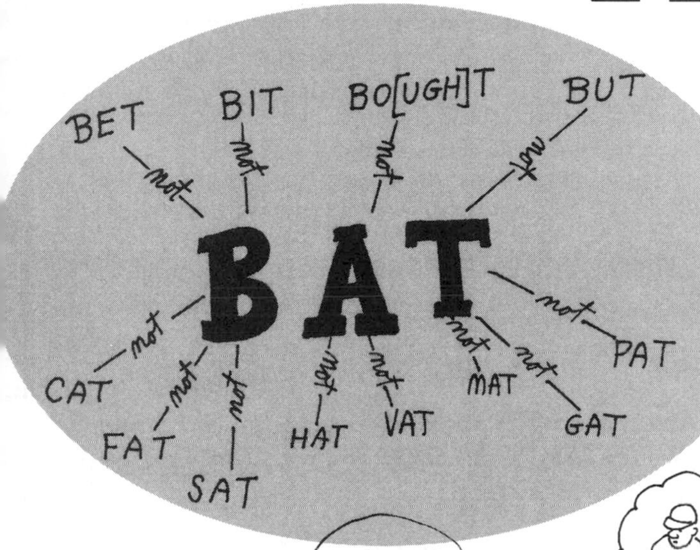

In each case the sound produced creates a distinct word. Consider the first of these words, "BAT." It is what it is by <u>not</u> being the words "bet," "bit," "bot" ["bought"], "but."

BET — not
BIT — not
BO[UGH]T — not
BUT — not

BAT

CAT — not
FAT — not
SAT — not
HAT — not
VAT — not
MAT — not
GAT — not
PAT — not

Sometimes people with foreign accents are misunderstood because they do not make these distinctions clear enough.

HE'S A <u>BAT</u> BOY!

SHE MEANS "BAD"

THEIR MOST PRECISE CHARACTERISTIC IS BEING WHAT THE OTHERS ARE NOT.

And what's true of SOUNDS is true of IDEAS.

Therefore

☞ (AND THIS IS RADICAL),

different languages produce different concepts. The French speaker not only <u>speaks</u> differently from the American, but THINKS differently. (Jonathan Culler, a Saussure scholar, has come up with an excellent example. In English, we have two words: "river" and "stream." In French there are also two words, "fleuve" and "riviére." Now it <u>looks</u> as if "river" and riviére should be identical but "fleuve" turns out to mean "river," even though our word "river" obviously evolved from the French "riviére." But in fact it is even more complicated than this. In English, "rivers" are bigger bodies of flowing water; streams by comparison are smaller. But in French, "fleuves" flow into the sea, and "riviéres" flow into "fleuves." So, STRICTLY SPEAKING, there is no word in English that means the same as the French words "fleuve" and "riviére.")

SHALL WE GO TO THE RIVER?

EH? WHAT? I DON'T UNDERSTAND A WORD YOU'RE SAYING!

Says Saussure:

READY-MADE IDEAS DO NOT EXIST BEFORE WORDS.

According to Saussure, language is made up of SIGNS. A sign is the combination of a SIGNIFIER (a "sound" or a "sound-image," like the noise "kAT") and a SIGNIFIED (an idea, a concept, for example, "any of several members of the family <u>Felidae</u>, but particularly the domesticated carnivore <u>Felis</u> <u>domestica</u>").

The first principle of Saussure's linguistics is THE ARBITRARINESS of THE SIGN. This means several things. First, there is no natural connection between the signifier and the signified. (Plato was wrong about that.) There are only <u>conventional</u> relations between words and meanings. There is nothing in nature nor in logic that <u>requires</u> that English speakers use the word "dog" for dogs.

19

There are partial exceptions. Words like "writing desk" are not purely arbitrary, even though both "writing" and "desk" are arbitrary. There is a kind of logical connection between the two words that link them. (Saussure called these terms "motivated.") Still, we shouldn't be too far misled by the "logic" of these "motivated" terms.

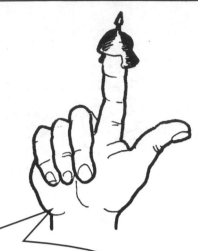

> FOR EXAMPLE, THE GERMANS CALL A THIMBLE A "FINGERHUT" (FINGER-HAT).

"Fingerhut" may be motivated, but "thimble" is not.

Also, so-called ONOMATOPOEIA are partially "motivated." These are words that are supposed to imitate sounds in nature, such as the English word "chirp." But in French a chirp is a "pépier" (like "peep!") and a "Zirp" in German. "Clap" in French is "claque," and in German "Knall." These are all onomatopoetic, but do they really "imitate nature?" Dogs say "bow-wow" in America, "bau-bau" in Italy, and "ouâ-ouâ" in France.

PLATO SEEMS TO HAVE HELD THE STRANGE VIEW THAT <u>ALL</u> WORDS WERE SOMEHOW ONOMATOPOETIC. THEY <u>IMITATED</u> REALITY.

CHIRP

BETTER WATCH OUT! IT'S PIGEON SEASON

Furthermore, for Saussure the <u>conventions</u> that tie t signifier to the signified ar also arbitrary. That mean that they, too, are determined not by facts in "real ty" but by other facts in t linguistic system, as we sa with the "river/riviére" exan ple. (The English word "pigeon" comes from the Latin word "pipio," a "chirp." The English word "dove" comes from the Gothic wc "dubo," meaning "diver."

But not all chirpers and divers are members of the family of birds known scientifically as "<u>Columbidae</u>," and anyway, I always thought that doves "cooed," not chirped.) What all this means is that there are no essences, "no fixed universal concepts." (Plato was wrong about <u>that</u> too.)

WRONG TWICE IN TWO PAGES?

Another important distinction in Saussurian linguistics is that between LA LANGUE (language) and PARÔLE (speech). "La langue" is the whole linguistic system. It is a social structure into which the individual is born. "Parôle" is composed of the actual speech acts that the speaker enunciates. It is the individual aspect of language rather than the social. "Parôle" must be analyzed in terms of "langue." Saussure compares "parôle" with an individual move in a chess game. It can only be understood in terms of the underlying system of rules which is chess. Yet at the primary level the rules govern only differences. The pawn is <u>not</u> the queen, the queen is <u>not</u> the bishop, the bishop is <u>not</u>...,etc. Furthermore, the queen is not defined by "her" material construction (ivory, wood, plastic) nor by her shape.

WE CAN REPLACE "HER" WITH ANYTHING AS LONG AS WE DON'T CONFUSE THAT OBJECT WITH THE OTHER PIECES.

In this comparison between language and chess we see the beginnings of a STRUCTURAL analysis rather than a CAUSAL analysis of the type used in the natural sciences. Neither a linguistic component nor a piece in chess is explained by showing what caused them, but by locating them within the structure of a system.

The distinction between "la langue" and "parôle" is related to another Saussurean dichotomy that has already been mentioned— that between a SYNCHRONIC and a DIACHRONIC study of language. The latter is the study of the evolution of language, of history's impact on linguistic events. The former is the study of all the relations among the different parts of a linguistic system at any given moment in time, without reference to the past. For Saussure, the major task of linguistic analysis is synchronic. The diachronic (historical) features are not the most important considerations for him.

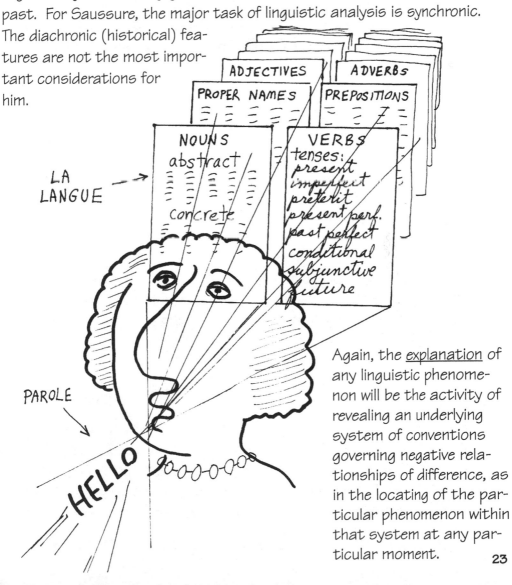

Again, the explanation of any linguistic phenomenon will be the activity of revealing an underlying system of conventions governing negative relationships of difference, as in the locating of the particular phenomenon within that system at any particular moment.

23

Another Saussurean distinction that will appear again in later structuralist writers is that between ASSOCIATIVE RELATIONS (today called PARADIGMS) and SYNTAGMS. Paradigmatic analysis is "vertical." It studies the rules of substitution within a particular grammatical category. Syntagmatic analysis is "horizontal." It studies temporal relations of contiguity.

The — { dog cat mouse } { eats observes rejects } **its** { meal. mate. dish. }

The horizontal substitutions are syntagmatic.
The vertical substitutions are paradigmatic.

Saussure's STRUCTURALISM can be seen most clearly in his claim that the whole of language as he wishes to study it can be displayed as a system of syntagmatic and paradigmatic negative relations of difference.

Ferdinand de Saussure's science of linguistics is a radical departure from the past, because it entails a whole new picture of the human mind. The mind is not, as the empiricists believed, a receptacle for sense-data from which it constructs a picture of the world piece by piece. Nor is the mind merely a system of innate ideas that are activated by sense-data, as the rationalists thought. Rather, the mind is a system of operations that generate structures of similarity and differentiation in terms of such rules as those of syntagmatic and paradigmatic relationships. It is because of these operations that MEANING is possible— that one thing can signify another.

Saussure's science is also radical because of the way it seems to overthrow realism (the view that there is a real world out there that can be known by the human mind) and to replace it with a linguistic relativism (what we can know is the system of concepts generated by the arbitrary structures of language).

And finally, it is radical in the way it seems to demote human individuality and freedom in the social world. Language cannot be interfered with by individuals.

> THE INDIVIDUAL DOES NOT HAVE THE POWER TO CHANGE A SIGN IN ANY WAY ONCE IT HAS BECOME ESTABLISHED IN THE LINGUISTIC COMMUNITY

In fact, when Saussure turns once again to the comparison between language and chess, he says that the analogy would be completely correct only if we could imagine an "unconscious or unintelligent player."

UNCONSCIOUS CHESS PLAYERS

In the Introduction to the _Course in General Linguistics_ Saussure calls for the development of a new science of SEMIOLOGY, the study of signs, of which linguistics would be a part, but social institutions themselves would be treated as systems of signs.

Perhaps it is the **STRUCTURAL ANTHROPOLOGY** of Claude Lévi-Strauss that picks up this challenge.

CLAUDE LEVI-STRAUSS
(b.1908)
pronounced "Levee-Strose"
(rhyming with "dose")

The two traditions in anthropology are, roughly, speculative and empirical. The speculative tradition is modeled on the work of Sir James Frazer (1854-1941), the Scottish folklorist whose office at the turn of the century was filled with hundreds of files containing information about "exotic cultures" sent to him by missionaries, tradespeople, sailors, colonists, and world travelers. Frazer's genius was that of <u>synthesizer</u>. He would go through his files, finding curious similarities among cultures in disparate parts of the world, then produce general theories about "primitive man."

FRAZER

ARMCHAIR ANTHROPOLOGY

Despite writing riveting bestsellers like <u>The Golden Bough</u> (1890), Frazer's style of armchair anthropology has been despised by the majority of professional anthropologists during the last three-quarters of this century. Their work has been modeled on the more empirical method of Bronislaw Malinowski (1884-1942), who lived four years "among the natives" of the Melanesian Islands of the Pacific, keeping detailed records of minute observations of the people and institutions in the specific locale where he planted himself.

This technique has produced a form of anthropology generally known as FUNCTIONALISM, which tries to demonstrate that "curious" and "exotic" behaviors and institutions actually have important social functions.

A BLESSING ON YOUR HEAD

Hindu worship of cattle not only provides spiritual warmth but physical warmth as well, as it allows the use of dried cow dung as fuel in a region where wood and oil are scarce.

PSSST! YOU WANNA BUY SOME ANTHROPOLOGY?

THE SEXUAL LIFE OF SAVAGES

The empirically-minded anthropologists have been generally satisfied to produce monographs and ethnographies covering only the details of the specific peoples they study. They are less interested in issuing broad generalizations about human nature in the style of James Frazer (though Malinowski did issue potboilers with titles like The Sexual Life of Savages [1929].)

Lévi-Strauss's work is in some ways the heir of Frazer's tradition. He disdains "sterile empiricism," he has never lived and studied among indigenous peoples for a sustained period, and he looks for universal principles true of all peoples at all times. Despite the many differences among cultures, they are all the creation of the human brain, so beneath their surfaces, there must be a basic character common to all cultures. Lévi-Strauss disagrees with the functionalist assumption that social phenomena must be explained by finding their hidden utilitarian functions. Some important forms of behavior have no literal utility at all. Their significance is revealed only when they are related negatively to other social phenomena in the same cultural system (like Saussure's "signifiers").

But let's say a word about Lévi-Strauss himself. He is Belgian by birth, born into an intellectually endowed French Jewish family. His grandfather was a rabbi in Versailles, near Paris, and it was there that he grew up. As a youth he was interested in music, literature, and the sciences, particularly geology.

IT'S ONLY A ROCK...

WOW!

FAR OUT!

EXCELLENT!

When he first read Freud and Marx he saw similarities between geology and their theories, each involving the need to excavate hidden stratifications.

HE WOULD LATER CALL MARX, FREUD AND GEOLOGY HIS "THREE MISTRESSES."

GRANITE

When he entered the University of Paris he studied law and philosophy, but he enjoyed reading anthropology books more than he enjoyed his studies. In 1934, a friend offered him the post of professor of sociology at São Paulo University in Brazil, which he immediately accepted. During the next four years Lévi-Strauss took jaunts into the Amazon jungle, where he made the acquaintance of several native tribes. Seeking the proverbial "state of nature" he discovered instead a form of native sophistication about which he began to theorize.

By then World War II had broken out, and rather than return to Paris, Lévi-Strauss found himself in New York where he was befriended by the Russian linguist Roman Jakobson, who passed on to Lévi-Strauss his enthusiasm for Saussure's theory of language. After the war, Lévi-Strauss returned to Paris, which became the base for his new synthesis of Freud, Marx, geology, Saussure, and the primitive sophistication of the Nambikwara Indians.

He called it "structuralism."

Lévi-Strauss's search for universals not only associates him with the anthropological tradition of James Frazer but also with the rationalistic philosophical tradition that began with Plato and was perfected by Immanuel Kant (1724-1804) in his search for "synthetic *a priori*" truths (universal truths that made perceptual truths possible but could not themselves be perceptual truths). Lévi-Strauss's version of this pursuit is his claim that universal human truths exist at the level of STRUCTURE, but are camouflaged at the level of observable fact unless one knows how to decode those facts.

(As was mentioned, Marx and Freud had said something similar.)

Lévi-Strauss studies that underlying social structure the same way Saussure had studied "la langue," as we see when we inspect Lévi-Strauss's statement of his method:

1. "Define the phenomenon under study as a relation between two or more terms, real or supposed;

2. "construct a table of possible permutations between these terms;

3. "take this table as the general object of analysis which... can yield necessary connections, the empirical phenomenon... being only one possible combination among others." Saussure had argued that people are born into linguistic systems that are already in place. Individuals had the freedom to organize the linguistic units in novel ways ("parôle"), but had no influence on the underlying basic structure ("langue").

PERIODIC CHART OF POSSIBLE SOCIAL RELATIONS
CHART ＊73a - SIBLINGS (SISTERS)

SISTER TO MOTHER	SISTER TO FATHER	SISTER TO OLDER BROTHER	SISTER TO YOUNGER BROTHER
SISTER TO OLDER SISTER	SISTER TO YOUNGER SISTER	SISTER TO GRAND-MOTHER	SISTER TO GRAND-FATHER
SISTER TO UNCLE	SISTER TO AUNT	SISTER TO FEMALE COUSIN	SISTER TO MALE COUSIN
SISTER TO STEP-SISTER	SISTER TO STEP-BROTHER	SISTER TO TWIN	SISTER TO GODMOTHER

> Human societies, like individual human beings... never create absolutely; all they can do is create certain combinations.

Lévi-Strauss said the same thing about cultural systems:

In finding common denominators in all human thought, Lévi-Strauss does serious damage to the Western prejudice about so-called "primitive peoples." In a book ironically titled in English translation, The Savage Mind, he tries to show that there is no such thing as a "savage mind." (A better translation of La pensée sauvage [1962] would be "Thinking in the Raw.") The old myth that primitive people are like children and think in some pre-logical manner is challenged with a two-pronged argument. First, there are features of "primitive thinking" that are demonstrated as being far more "technical" and subtle than our own, and second, there are areas of "cultured thought" that are revealed as being extremely "primitive."

> WHAT AM I OFFERED FOR THIS FINE DUST-BALL FROM ELVIS'S HOUSE?

CELEBRITY AUCTION

As examples of the latter, consider certain monuments, like Mount Rushmore, our collections of signed baseballs, the small replicas of the Eiffel Tower we bring back as "souvenirs" of our trip to Paris, the plastic flowers we put on graves, the useless objects purchased at auctions because they once belonged to famous people.

As examples of "hi-tech" primitive thought, Lévi-Strauss catalogues hundreds of sophisticated systems of classification of natural objects by native peoples. For instance, the Hanunoo of the Philippine Islands have a botanical vocabulary dividing local plants into more than 1800 mutually exclusive categories, while Western botanists divide the same group into fewer than 1300 categories. The Hanunoo also distinguish among 60 kinds of fish, 108 kinds of insects, 60 classes of salt water molluscs and 25 molluscs found on land or in sweet water.

However, the Hanunoo are <u>not</u> able to distinguish between chardonnay and chablis.

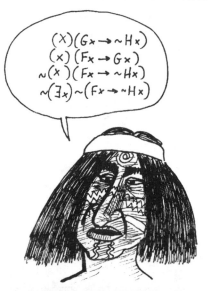

$$(X)(Gx \rightarrow \sim Hx)$$
$$(x)(Fx \rightarrow Gx)$$
$$\sim(x)(Fx \rightarrow \sim Hx)$$
$$\sim(\exists x)\sim(Fx \rightarrow \sim Hx)$$

The classificatory categories of indigenous peoples are <u>logical</u> types, Lévi-Strauss tries to demonstrate. Like our own categories (and like Saussure's "phonemes") they are based on the recognition of opposites, contrasts and similarities. Moreover, they reveal a mastery of the immediate sensory qualities of the world, and an intuitive capacity for detecting analogues within combinations of sounds, colors, tastes, odors, and tactile qualities found in nature.

In fact, the "savage mind" is applying a universal human logic to resolve the problems posed by nature. We can discover the unity of the human race by studying this logic in its purest form— as it appears in the "unpolluted" mind of pre-industrial peoples.

TRUTH AT THE LEVEL OF CONSCIOUSNESS

YOU DESERVE SOMETHING NICE

OH, HOW SWEET OF YOU

TRUTH AT THE LEVEL OF STRUCTURE

ESTABLISHMENT OF A SYSTEM OF RECIPROCITY AND MUTUAL OBLIGATION

In his book The Elementary Structures of Kinship (1949), Lévi-Strauss carries out his Saussurean program of demonstrating that cultural phenomena should be treated as "signs." The anthropological inspiration for this work was Marcel Mauss's The Gift (1924). Lévi-Strauss reports that when he read this pioneering work of proto-structuralism his heart throbbed and his head seethed. Mauss had claimed that the institution of gift-giving was the basic organizational structure of all societies, that the exchange of gifts, regardless of the intention behind them or of what they consisted, established a system of mutual obligation that made society possible.

I WANNA MARRY MY SISTER

RIDICULOUS

Levi-Strauss takes Mauss's theory of gift exchange and applies it to the exchange of words, but also to the exchange of women (fathers and brothers "marrying off" their daughters and sisters). The near universality of the incest taboo is explained in terms of this exchange, which generates certain necessary kinship systems. Incest must be excluded from all such systems because it negates the establishment of social alliances. According to Lévi-Strauss, among "primitives" incest is not thought of as morally outrageous, but as socially ridiculous.

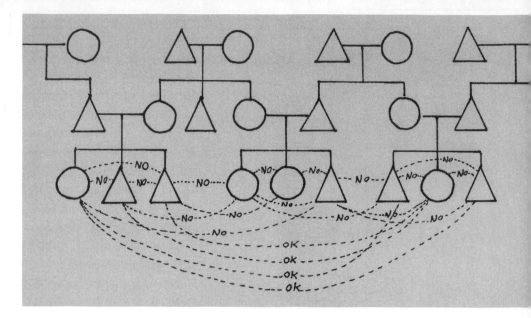

AN AMAZONIAN EXCHANGE OF MALES—
ONE POSSIBLE PERMUTATION OF THE FORMULA

The exchange of women is the most aboriginal form of exchange, because both the symbol and the entity symbolized are identical. Other forms of exchange are derivatives of this original form. (To the charge that his theory is sexist, Lévi-Strauss responds that the exchange of men rather than of women could have taken place in principle— that is to say, it is one of the "possible permutations" available— but that in fact it just didn't work out that way.)

Again, cultural phenomena should be treated as SIGNS. In Elementary Structures, Lévi-Strauss attempts to show that kinship relations are like linguistic systems, with members of society standing in a binary relationship of opposition and correlation to each other, much as do linguistic signs to one another. The members are like repertoires of exchange, and the rules of exchange are like a grammar. Within a set of binary opposites (left/right, male/female, permitted/forbidden) individuals communicate by a system of exchange. They exchange signs, all derived from the original sexual exchange.

A specific version of this general theory is found in Lévi-Strauss's attempt to solve what is known by anthropologists as "THE PROBLEM OF THE AVUNCU-LATE." This concerns the relation between a boy and his maternal uncle. Often they have a unique bond: either the boy fears the uncle and obeys his will unquestioningly, or the two have a "joking relation-ship" of informality. According to Lévi-Strauss, most attempts to explain these phenomena fail because they only treat the two individuals in question and do not locate them in a larger context of relationships. Lévi-Strauss discov-

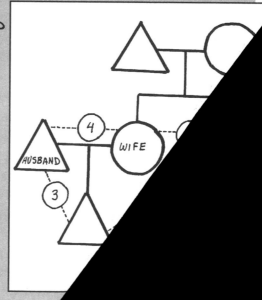

YOUR UNCLE SAM WANTS YOU

ers that the avunculate is a "global system" involving relations among four persons: son, father, mother, and uncle. The structure of this relationship can be stated as a formula:

The relation between [1] maternal uncle and nephew is to the relation between [2] brother and sister as the relation between [3] father and son is to that between [4] husband and wife."

That is, [1] is to [2] as [3] is to [4].

If [1] and [4] are harmonious then [2] and [3] are dis-tant... (as among the Tonga of Polynesia).

If [2] and [3] are harmonious then [1] and [4] are dis-tant... (as among the Siuai of the former Congo).

Lévi-Strauss has also applied his structuralist method to the knotty problem of "totemism" in a book of the same title (<u>Totemism</u>, 1962). Travelers, missionaries, and anthropologists have noted for hundreds of years that certain "primitive" peoples have organized themselves into clans and moities that they believe to have derived from some supernatural animal (the "totem") which they worship as an ancestor. Of course anthropologists have been fascinated by this phenomenon, and have spent an inordinate amount of energy trying to explain it. In 1920, a book was published distinguishing forty-one theories of ~~~ism. Probably the most famous example is Freud's attempt in ~~~boo (1913) to show that totemism derives from the ~~~tion of the repressed memory of the "Primal ~~~ social history.

ual treatment of
ing ODD— something
t, totemism is an
s. Gleaning insights
a social extension of
terms of METAPHOR
in which there is a sub-
on recognition of SIMI-
e's "syntagm," in which there
contiguity, or in terms of
le) depends on CONTINUITY.

Letting animals stand for humans is metaphor. Describing animals as extensions of humans is metonymy. The relation between the clan and its totem is not literal but analogical. Members of the eagle clan do not look or act like eagles, nor do members of the bear clan look or live like bears. But eagles and bears live at different heights and move at different speeds. So clans <u>differ</u> from one another in analogous ways— they use different masks and reside at different ground levels of the village.

It is not the resemblances, but the differences, which resemble each other

TOTEMISM IS THE SYSTEM THAT ISOLATES THESE ANALOGOUS DIFFERENCES BETWEEN GROUPS OF HUMANS AND GROUPS OF ANIMALS.

This is the way totemism works, and this is the way the human mind works. The mind not only perceives location, height, and depth but also <u>relationships</u> of <u>contrast.</u> This is a human universal. The mind looks for analogies in various realms and encompasses them into systems. Consciously we perceive THINGS, but unconsciously we perceive RELATIONSHIPS. The mind meditates upon these relationships and generates pictures of the world based on their systematization. "Totemic animals are chosen not because they are 'good to eat' but because they are good to think."

Like Freud, but for very different reasons, Lévi-Strauss finds reverberations of totemism in "civilized" thought. For example, pet birds tend to have names borrowed from the lexicon of human names (Peter, Bill, Suzy). On the contrary, dogs tend to be given names that are in odd ways like human names but ultimately are non-human (Fido, Bowser, Fifi). Why can we afford to give human names to birds but are less willing to give them to dogs, even though both are kept around the house? Because birds inhabit their own parallel but quite separate society (and hence are METAPHORICAL HUMANS), while dogs are an extension of the family (hence are METONYMICAL HUMANS). We do not need to distinguish birds from ourselves, so we can afford to grant them human names, but in order to preserve the distinction between ourselves and dogs at some level, we cannot afford to give them in every instance truly human names.

SOME EXCEPTIONS CAN BE TOLERATED.

Racehorses and cattle both are excluded from the human home, but inhabit a human world. Why are the names we give these two groups so different from those of birds and dogs? In the case of cows, there is no interest in the individual identities, but only in their general utility, so names, if they are given at all, are general. ("Bossie".) Racehorses on the contrary, are of interest because of their individual differences. Their names will emphasize their distinctiveness or their owner's cleverness. ("Man o' War," "Seabiscuit".)

BOVINE INDIVIDUALISM

In summarizing all this Lévi-Strauss says:

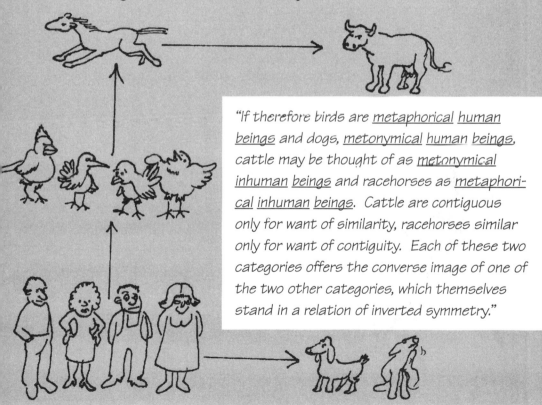

"If therefore birds are <u>metaphorical</u> <u>human</u> <u>beings</u> and dogs, <u>metonymical</u> <u>human</u> <u>beings</u>, cattle may be thought of as <u>metonymical</u> <u>inhuman</u> <u>beings</u> and racehorses as <u>metaphorical</u> <u>inhuman</u> <u>beings</u>. Cattle are contiguous only for want of similarity, racehorses similar only for want of contiguity. Each of these two categories offers the converse image of one of the two other categories, which themselves stand in a relation of inverted symmetry."

Once again, we see the formula: A is to B as C is to D, and the universal human ability to detect similarity in difference. Realizing this, we can study totemism and see that the descriptions of animal events are algebraic transformations of human events.

41

THE MIND IS NOT ONLY COG-
NIZANT OF OPPOSITIONS, BUT
IT MUST <u>MEDIATE</u> THEM ALSO,
SO SOME OF THE TOTEMIC ANI-
MALS THAT ARE "GOOD TO
THINK" WILL BE MEDIATORS—
THAT IS, ANIMALS WITH OPPOS-
ING CHARACTERISTICS. THIS
EXPLAINS THE COMMONALITY OF
TRICKSTERS AND **JOKERS** IN
"PRIMITIVE" MYTHICAL SYS-
TEMS, WHO HAVE A BIT OF THE
SUPERNATURAL BUT ALSO A BIT
OF THE RIDICULOUS. THINK OF
COYOTE AND RAVEN IN SOME
NATIVE AMERICAN MYTHS.

Lévi-Strauss's application of the method of structural linguistics to the study of myth has produced four volumes of his <u>Mythologiques</u> (1964-

1972). According to him, in the process of myth-making, the mind is liberated from the necessity of dealing with external objects, and therefore it can reflect its own laws of operation; it can imitate itself as an object. Myths reveal the structure of the mind.

Furthermore, the mind, being a part of the universe, reflects in some way the structure of the universe. Therefore, the products of the mind, such as myths and languages, somehow reveal the nature of the world. Culture is a product of the human mind, which is itself a product of nature. The structural study of the artifacts of the mind reveals a relatively faithful reflection of the structure of reality. There is a homology between thought and its objects.

Myths function like languages, so mythology, like linguistics, must locate the basic units of myths (what Lévi-Strauss sometimes calls "mythemes") along with their unique characteristics and their rules of combination and exclusion.

However, in some ways myths are more like music than like language. Parts are duplicated with great frequency; there are many "variations on a theme," and the main elements "sink in" after repeated familiarity.

Then Cronos from his ambush sprang...

All configurations of human behavior are codes, which, when decoded, reveal themselves as attempted solutions of universal human dilemmas. Using the basic "mythemes" (categories of food, smells, tastes, sounds, silences, seasons, climates), myths express the contradictions of life in a structured pattern and render them intelligible. Myths function "to provide a logical model capable of overcoming a contradiction (an impossible achievement if, as it happens, the contradiction is real)."

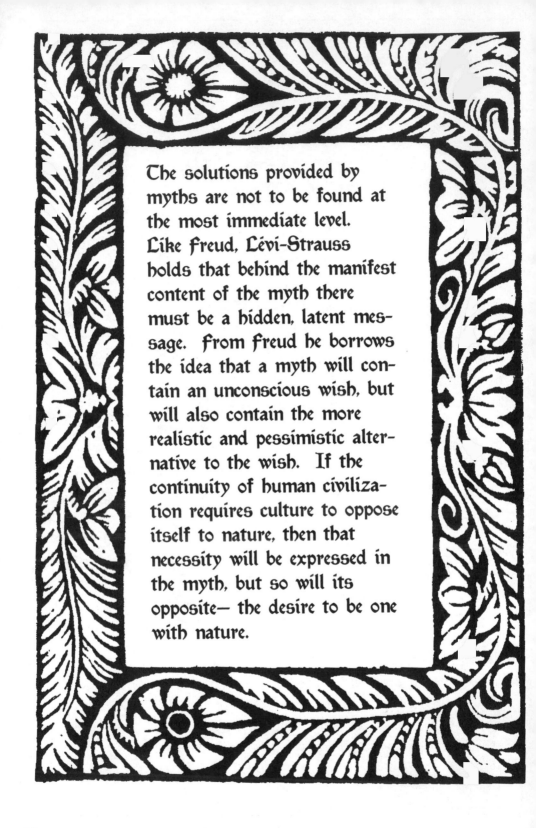

The solutions provided by myths are not to be found at the most immediate level. Like Freud, Lévi-Strauss holds that behind the manifest content of the myth there must be a hidden, latent message. From Freud he borrows the idea that a myth will contain an unconscious wish, but will also contain the more realistic and pessimistic alternative to the wish. If the continuity of human civilization requires culture to oppose itself to nature, then that necessity will be expressed in the myth, but so will its opposite— the desire to be one with nature.

Not only does Lévi-Strauss borrow from Freud, he also borrows from general information theory. The ancestors are the senders of the message. The members of the current generation are the receivers. The message is sent from a distance through heavy interference, so it must be repeated in a variety of manners. In order to decode the true message all the received messages must be overlaid, one on top of the other.

Such a decoding of an aboriginal message can be found if we look at the Straussian analysis of the myth of Oedipus reconstructed by the staff of <u>Psychology</u> <u>Today</u> magazine (May, 1972), a simplified version of Lévi-Struass's more complicated rendition that appeared in his article,

"The Structural Study of Myth."

Reading from left to right we see that similar elements appear in each column. In columns A and B, "born from one" refers to the theme of being born from mother earth. In A, monsters "born of the earth" who endanger human existence are destroyed, so their power is denied. However, in B, the common denominator is lameness, which affirms the theme, "born of the earth, "because often in myths those who are so born are crippled and stumble. In columns C and D, we see the opposition between undervaluing and overvaluing blood ties.

A **DENIAL** (is to)	Man is not born of the earth (born from one).	Cadmus, founder of Thebes, slays a dragon. Its teeth, sown in the earth, turn into warriors. ①			
B **AFFIRMATION** (as)	Man is born of the earth (born from one).			The name of the next king, Labdacos, may mean "lame." The name of his son, Laios, may mean ③ "left-sided."	Oedipus (= "swollen foot") by leaving him to die with pins through his ankles. ⑤
C **DENIAL** (is to)	Ties of blood are <u>less</u> important than social relations.		who kill each other ②	Because of a prophecy, Laios tries to kill his infant son. ④	
D **AFFIRMATION**	Ties of blood are <u>more</u> important than social relations.				

The myth attempts to resolve a pair of contradictions present in the Greek mind by establishing a kind of formula. Once again, (A) is to (B) as (C) is to (D). This "solution" to the problem of culture versus nature may be emotionally satisfying, but in terms of a strictly logical scrutiny it fails. This is because, according to Lévi-Strauss, the dilemmas of human existence are based on <u>real</u> contradictions that cannot be overcome. He says pessimistically that myths are epics of inevitable human tragedy.

	slays the sphinx by solving the riddle, ⑦				
			Discovering his "crime", Oedipus blinds himself and is exiled He cannot walk without a guide. ⑨		
Oedipus kills his father, ⑥				The twin sons of Oedipus battle for Thebes and kill each other. ⑩	and dies as a result. ⑫
		and becomes king of Thebes by marrying his mother. ⑧			Antigone, Oedipus' daughter disobeys her uncle, the new king, by burying one of her brothers. ⑪

(after Maurice Henry)

The appearance in 1966 in a French review of literature of a cartoon by Maurice Henry that came to be known as "The Structuralists' Lunch Party" coincided with structuralism's rise to the top of the French intellectual scene and its triumph over the existentialism of Jean-Paul Sartre that had preceded it. The rough copy of Henry's drawing that you see here shows the best-known structuralists of the day, (Michel Foucault, Jacques Lacan, Claude Lévi-Strauss and Roland Barthes) wearing grass skirts against a tropical background.

Reviewing the fields of each of the "picnickers" in the cartoon shows how broad is the scope of structuralism. We've already seen that Lévi-Strauss is an anthropologist. Foucault is a philosopher and historian, Lacan is a psychoanalyst, and Barthes a literary critic.

We will now turn to the thought of each of these structuralist theorists (some of whom soon became "post-structuralists").

ROLAND BARTHES

(1915-1980)

pronounced "BART"

*B*arthes was born during World War I in Bayonne, on the southern Atlantic coast of France. His father was killed in action when Roland was only a year old, so he was raised by his mother and aunts. When he was nine years old, Roland moved with his mother to Paris, where she took a poorly paid job as a bookbinder. He remained there through his school and university years.

His poor health exempted him from military service, and he spent World War II in tuberculosis sanitoria in the Alps. After the war he taught and wrote, his books earning him renown by 1965, when he was recognized as one of the movers and shakers of the new structuralist movement. He was given a professorship at the esteemed Collége de France in Paris in 1977. His life came to an end in 1980 when he was struck by a laundry truck while crossing the street in front of the college.

As a theorist, Barthes was never very faithful to any one point of view. He flitted from Sartrean existentialism to Marxism to structuralism, then to hedonism, often attacking his earlier views as he moved away from them. Still, there are certain constants that last throughout his work. First, from Sartre he derived a dislike for ESSENTIALISM.

BUZZZ

"Essentialism" is a belief in the priority of "essences." An essence would be something like a Platonic Form—— a definition, a formula, a set of characteristics that stabilizes objects in the world. We have already seen that the essence of a triangle is that which all triangles have in common, "triangularity." The essence of humans is that which they all have in common, "humanity."

The motto of Sartre's existentialism was "existence precedes essence," by which he meant that there is no such thing as a human essence or a human nature that determines what and who we must be. But Barthes goes beyond Sartre, who seemed to allow that objects other than human beings might have essences.

OH, YOU'RE JUST SO MIDDLE CLASS!

But for Barthes, there are no essences at all. Essentialism is just a bourgeois ideology attempting to squeeze reality into its own mold and freeze-dry it there. (Never mind that Plato, who was hardly bourgeois, was the first essentialist.)

There are for Barthes no unities, only pluralities. In fact, Barthes claimed to look forward to the dissolution of his own physical being into dust and memories in the minds of his friends.

Another related Barthean constant is his attack on "the voice of the natural" in cultural phenomena. There is a tendency for the dominating social forces to generate the myth that the rules, mores, and institutions of that society are "nature's way" (or, in an earlier generation, "God's way"). The implication is that these moral codes and institutions cannot be called into question except by "perverts." As we shall see, this view is thoroughly demolished by Barthes' caustic wit.

A third feature of Barthes' work that is constant at least after his earliest writings is his commitment to a Saussurean vocabulary and a radicalization of Saussure's meanings. There are no essences; there is no nature in the human world. There aren't even any "facts." What exists for us are SIGNS, and systems of encoding and decoding signs. There can be no innocent presentations of the human world. There are only guilty signs that create their own facts.

Despite the many phases of Barthes's career as a literary critic, he is best known for his STRUCTURALIST and SEMIOLOGICAL views (two terms that are roughly equivalent in his work). In his <u>Elements</u> <u>of</u> <u>Semiology</u> (1964), he accepted Saussure's challenge to commence a "science of semiology," applying to cultural phenomena Saussure's categories:

☞ language and speech (<u>la</u> <u>langue</u> and <u>le</u> <u>parole</u>)

☞ signified and signifier,

☞ syntagm and paradigm.

For example, he treats the "world of fashion" as a system of signs: "This year flower prints will show a hint of elegance." (The signifier is the flower print dress. The signified is "elegance.")

IT'S NOT THAT THE ELEGANT WEAR FLOWER PRINTS. IT'S THAT FLOWER PRINTS MAKE YOU ELEGANT.

And the food industry is dealt with as a semiological system: "A mousse? Made with margarine? Unthinkable!" (The signifier is the image of the mousse. The signified is the invitation to overcome economic prejudice by purchasing a new product.)

Barthes's structuralism is even more creative in his book <u>Sade/Fourier/Loyola</u> (1971). It is typical of Barthes that he would be interested in three such incongruous writers, and quite amazing that he produces a "grammar" of their writings, reducing them to their basic elements and laying out the rules of combination of these elements, much as Lévi-Strauss did with kinship relationships. The Marquis de Sade catalogues all possible sexual adventures.

François Fourier invents the elemental units of a socialist utopia and the rules of their combination, and Ignatius Loyola, founder of the Jesuit Order, sets down the elements and rules of spiritual discipline. Barthes finds in all of them the same tendency to create systems of distinction, ordering and classification.

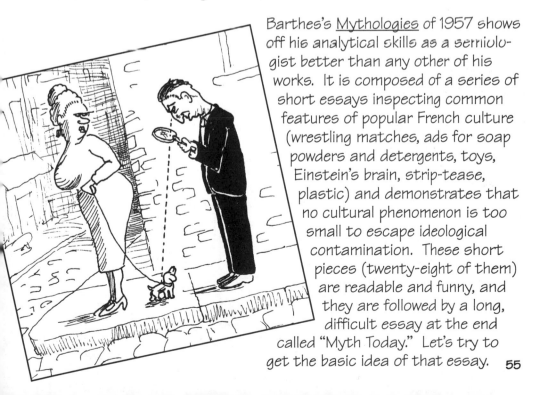

Barthes's <u>Mythologies</u> of 1957 shows off his analytical skills as a semiologist better than any other of his works. It is composed of a series of short essays inspecting common features of popular French culture (wrestling matches, ads for soap powders and detergents, toys, Einstein's brain, strip-tease, plastic) and demonstrates that no cultural phenomenon is too small to escape ideological contamination. These short pieces (twenty-eight of them) are readable and funny, and they are followed by a long, difficult essay at the end called "Myth Today." Let's try to get the basic idea of that essay. **55**

First, what Barthes means by "myth" is only distantly related to what Lévi-Strauss meant by the same word. It is much more closely related to Karl Marx's term "ideology," which is a form of (usually unconscious) political propaganda that is presented as fact while at the same time masking contradictions within the social system.

For instance, the slogan "All men are equal under the law" idealizes a certain political structure— namely, ours— at the same time that it disguises the social contradiction entailed by implying that the millionaire is as susceptible as the unemployed laborer to the law that prohibits stealing breadcrusts for one's starving children.

CRUSTS AGAIN?

SHUT UP AND EAT!

For Barthes, a myth is a form of discourse that tries to make cultural norms appear as facts of nature. Barthes demythologizes by revealing the semiological codes that myths employ.

Remind yourself of Saussure's theory of the SIGN. A sign is a combination of a <u>signifier</u> (the sound image or visual image) and the <u>signified</u> (the concept). For example, in our culture, ROSES can be a signifier for PASSION, which is the signified.

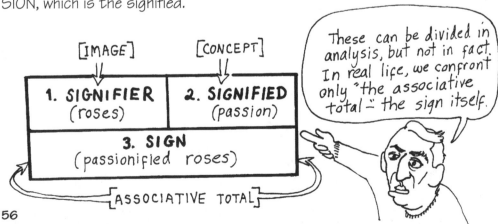

[IMAGE]   [CONCEPT]

1. SIGNIFIER (roses)	2. SIGNIFIED (passion)
3. SIGN (passionified roses)	

[ASSOCIATIVE TOTAL]

These can be divided in analysis, but not in fact. In real life, we confront only "the associative total"— the sign itself.

Now, according to Barthes, for most discourse, this model is sufficient, but in "myths" the sign itself becomes a signifier in a new system of meaning, creating "a second-order semiological system." For example, think of the function of the sign "passionified roses" when it enters into the semiological system involving advertizing for Valentine's Day purchases.

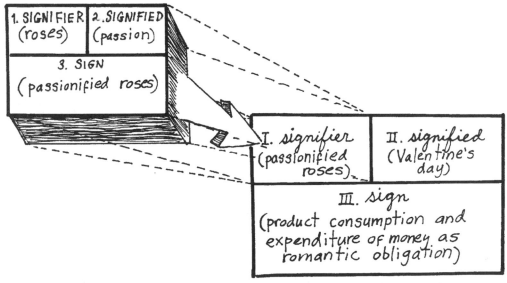

Here the original sign (now only a signifier) has become <u>emptied</u>, robbed of its meaning. It has been expropriated and alienated from its users.

A famous example of Barthes's is the following: He is sitting in a barber's shop looking at <u>Paris Match</u>, a popular French magazine. On the cover a young black soldier is saluting, his eyes looking upward, presumably at the French flag. This is the signifier. The signified is "Frenchness and militarism," the total sign is all of this (faithful black French soldier).

But in the <u>mythical</u> semiological system, the <u>new</u> sign says something like this: "France is a great Empire... all her sons, without any colour discrimination, faithfully serve under her flag... there is no better answer to the detractors of an alleged colonialism than the zeal shown by this Negro in serving his so-called oppressors."

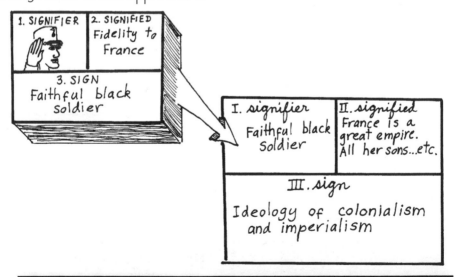

So here the true meaning of the original sign is distorted by being emptied of its history.

Barthes concludes:

It is now possible to complete the semiological definition of myth in a bourgeois society: MYTH IS DEPOLITICIZED SPEECH.

For Barthes, the only speech that cannot be "depoliticized" and mythologized is "speech which is the opposite of myth: that which remains political." Basically, only revolutionary language escapes myth.

So we see that, at least in 1957, Barthes' structuralism/semiology is still linked to his early Marxism. (Looking back at it now, his idea that leftist myth is essentially impossible seems itself to be mythological.) Yet, by perusing the short "mythologies" in Barthes's book, we see that myths are not necessarily complete deceptions. For example, in the article called "Wine and Milk," Barthes connects the 'Frenchness' of wine with capitalism and exploitation; nevertheless he admits...

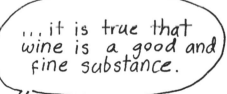

...it is true that wine is a good and fine substance.

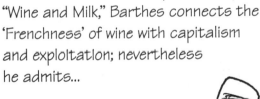

In his article, "The World of Wrestling," the popularity of wrestling matches is derived from their ability to signify ideas like those of Justice, Good, and Evil as part of the Natural Order. These are obviously mythical ideas in Barthes' sense. Yet, rather than condemning wrestling, Barthes is obviously celebrating it as a spectacle of excess. He praises the "absolute clarity" of its signs, which are the bodies themselves of the wrestlers. He says, "There is no more a problem of truth in wrestling than in the theatre." It is not a sadistic spectacle, as some of its critics claim; it is an intelligible spectacle.

*I*t gives the audience what it wants: not passion, but the **IMAGE** of passion.

As a literary critic, one of Barthes's most dramatic moves was to divide all authors into two types, what he calls ECRIVANTS and ECRIVAINS. The former means roughly "writers," and the latter "authors." Barthes is much less interested in "writers/ecrivants," who use language for extra-linguistic ends; that is, their writing serves as a medium for achieving a moral, political, or practical goal.

Because for them language is only a tool, what they say is intended to have one and only one meaning. "Ecrivains" (authors) on

These writers are mere clerks.

the other hand are more "noble." They are interested in WORDS, not THINGS. Ecrivains produce not works, but TEXTS.

A true text is a kind of carnival of words, where, as in Mardi Gras, things normally prohibited are allowed. Speaking of language in 1960 the way he spoke of wrestling in 1957, Barthes says that a "text" is a LINGUISTIC SPECTACLE. A "text" is more interested in SIGNIFIERS than in SIGNIFIEDS. The ecrivain takes care of the signifiers and lets the signifieds take care of themselves.

Usually "writers" ("ecrivants") produce "the classics," and "authors" ("ecrivains") produce avant-garde works that Barthes happens to like (Bertolt Brecht, Phillipe Sollers, Alain Robbe-Grillet). He says that the nearest thing we have to a true "Text" is James Joyces's <u>Finnegan's Wake</u>, which is often excoriated as being an impossible book with no meaning at all.

"...it is not a miseffectual whyacinthinous riot of blots and blurs and bars and balls and hoops,"..... WHAT DOES IT ALL MEAN?

I never said it MEANT anything.

FINNEGAN'S WAKE

Later, in a book called <u>S/Z</u> (1970), Barthes drew a distinction similar to his <u>ecrivant</u>/<u>ecrivain</u> dichotomy, concentrating this time not on <u>authors</u> but on <u>texts</u>, dividing books into those that are <u>readerly</u> (<u>lisible</u>) and <u>writerly</u> (<u>scriptible</u>). "Readerly" works are again the type we find more familiar and easiest to read; "writerly" are resistant to easy reading, and Barthes prefers these. It looks as if his distinction once again pits avant-garde against classical works, but Barthes surprises us in <u>S/Z</u> (which is about Honoré de Balzac's short story "Sarrasine") by reading Balzac's story not as a "readerly" text but as a "writerly" one. It is as if Barthes is transforming Balzac from an <u>ecrivant</u> into an <u>ecrivain</u> before our very eyes, and thereby rescuing him from rigor mortis by finding layerings of ambiguity and plurality where before only univocality (single meaning) was seen. Barthes had performed a similar rescue operation on the work of the traditionalist patriotic historian of the nineteenth century, Jules Michelet. From him, Barthes had copied out onto a pile of cards phrases and sentences that pleased him. He scattered the cards about and rearranged them into a new text with new meanings.

For Barthes, no text can have just one meaning; and the more meanings, the better it is. Barthes demythologizes the great French literary ideal of lucidity (<u>clarté</u>), showing that it is not at all a natural goal of all good writing or correct thinking, but rather a piece of bourgeois ideology derived from the French courts in the seventeenth century, where it becomes a tool of manipulation and an exercise of power.

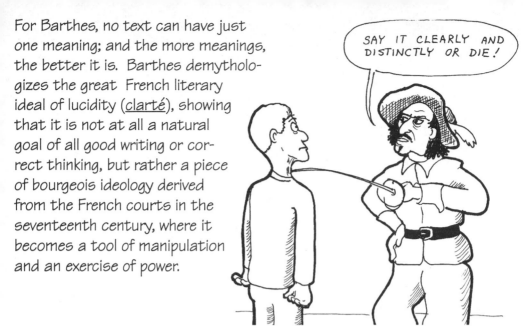

Literature for Barthes is not the bearer of meaning but a <u>critique</u> of meaning. Literature, in refusing to assign any final meanings, can be shown to have an anti-theological mission that is truly revolutionary, because the refusal of fixed meanings is the refusal of God. Barthes does not argue that the authors of literary works necessarily <u>intended</u> this critique. In fact, the critique is at the expense of authors. Barthes talks about "the death of the author."

But the consequence of this death is "the birth of the reader." The announcement of this cycle of death and birth is consistent with the movement of Barthes's concern from the <u>ecrivain</u> (author) to the <u>texte scriptible</u> (writerly text).

In the last phase of his life, Barthes seemed to move away from structuralism and post-structuralism and from his earlier radical political and literary stances and into an unabashed hedonism. In The Pleasure of the Text (1973), he appears to have come full circle, as he praises the very qualities in literature that an earlier generation of critics had done. His exaltation of the pleasure taken in the appreciation of literary qualities makes him sound like a classical "man of letters" of the type for which he had earlier shown nothing but scorn. And in A Lover's Discourse: Fragments (1977), he praises the sentimentality of ordinary love.

Yet even this move reveals to us after all the old Barthes who had created a radical transgressive aesthetic. He shows this first of all insofar as his new "traditionalism" is parasitical upon his earlier, more radical views. It is like a Hegelian "sublation" of his former views— an incorporating of them and moving beyond them at the same time, rather than just a rejection of them. Also, to take something as apparently simplistic and absurd as sentimental love and to make it the object of acute interest is a form of transgression. Barthes himself sees this. Talking about the "politico-sexual discourse" that his own work has opened up and explored, he says:

... a touch of sentimentality; would that not be the ultimate transgression?

What he seemed to be attempting was to break the head-lock that the academicians had on classical literature, freeing it up not as knowledge but as pleasure.

JACQUES LACAN

(1901-1981)

pronounced "Jock La-con," with a slight "g" sound at the end-almost "la-cong."

*J*acques Lacan, was born in Paris. He came to his study of Freud with a medical degree and a psychiatric diploma in hand. Challenging the orthodox psychoanalytic institution, he soon found himself exiled from its circle. Thereupon he established his own psychoanalytic training academy, the "Ecole Freudienne de Paris." Despite the difficult nature of his writing and his lectures, his fame spread and soon eclipsed that of any member of the official French psychoanalytic establishment. After feuding with close associates in his own school, he left it in 1963 and became "chargé de Conferences" at the prestigious "Ecole Practique de Hautes Etudes." He died in 1981, having left his mark not only on psychoanalysis, but on sociology, philosophy, and literary criticism.

SAUSSURE AND FREUD

If "structuralism" turns out to be essentially the application of Saussurean linguistics to explain the inherent structure of all forms of human activity, including mental activity and pathological behavior, then the psychoanalyst Jacques Lacan is a structuralist. And if "post-structuralism" is the <u>radicalization</u> of Saussure's linguistics to challenge the notion of structural stability (more on this later), then Lacan is also a post-structuralist.

> If you want to know more, read Saussure.... I am referring to Ferdinand.

> TELL US WHEN YOU'D LIKE A LITTLE SILENCE

BLAH BLAH BLAH BLAH BLAH BLAH BLAH BLAH BLAH BLAH BLAH BLAH BLAH BLAH BLAH

Furthermore, he is a structuralist insofar as he uses Saussure to read Freud, but a post-structuralist in that he uses Freud to read Saussure. Lacan accepts from Saussure that language (<u>la langue</u>) is a structure that pre-exists the individual and is not in the control of the individual and indeed is one that determines the individual's possibilities. But Saussure thought there was freedom at least in individual speech-acts (<u>la parôle</u>). Sometimes Lacan seems to doubt even that.

He says:

The subject is spoken rather than speaking.

Lacan also accepts Saussure's distinction between the "paradigmatic" and "syntagmatic" functions of language.

REMINDER:

"Paradigmatic" is that **VERTICAL** feature of language whereby we can replace one term in a sentence with related terms. For example "HOUSE" can be replaced with "home," "shack," "hut," "tent," "apartment," "place" or "castle." "Syntagmatic" is the **HORIZONTAL** feature that allows us to transform sequences of words into sentences.

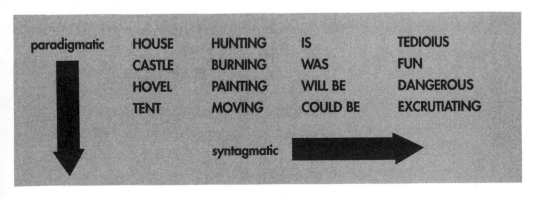

paradigmatic			
HOUSE	HUNTING	IS	TEDIOIUS
CASTLE	BURNING	WAS	FUN
HOVEL	PAINTING	WILL BE	DANGEROUS
TENT	MOVING	COULD BE	EXCRUTIATING

syntagmatic

But Lacan expands this, following ideas of the Russian linguist Roman Jakobson (1896-1982), transforming the idea of PARADIGM into that of METAPHOR, and the idea of SYNTAGM into that of METONOMY. (Metaphor is the replacement of one idea or image with another, or the collapsing of two such images or ideas together, e.g., "Achilles is a lion in battle."

ACHILLES

Metonymy is association by contiguity. That is, the whole standing for the part or the part standing for the whole, e.g., "A thousand sails set out to sea." But also, in Lacan's usage of the term, it is connection by rhyme, sound, or even free association.) The effect of this re-reading of Saussure is to make the poetic rather than the literal function of language its essential one.

Furthermore, by making metaphor and metonymy the two main poles of language, Lacan can recognize a basic unity between the structure of language and the structure of the unconscious, for Freud had claimed that the two main processes of unconscious thought were CONDENSATION (where for example in dreams a number of wish-laden images are collapsed into one

image and are thereby unrecognizable to the dreamer) and DISPLACEMENT (where a wish is deflected from its original forbidden object onto another whose relation to the first is unrecognized by the subject— like Freud's example of the woman who burns her lunch on the stove while reading a "Dear Jane" letter from her fiance, and thereafter the smell of burnt food causes a neurotic panic in her.) These two processes find their linguistic counterparts in metaphor and metonymy.

Lacan also adopts Saussure's vocabulary of the Sign, namely, "signifier" and "signified." Saussure had said that a signifier can be what it is only in contrast with other signifiers, but when looking at the meaning of a sign, Saussure inspected the relationship between the signifier (sound image) and the signified (concept). Lacan, however, seeks the meaning of signifiers in the relation to <u>other</u> signifiers. For him, what a signifier signifies is another signifier.

It's as if the meaning of a word in a specific sentence depends on its relationship to all the other words in it. Sometimes the last word or two in the sentence will alter the meaning of the other words retrospectively. (A lot of jokes are based on this fact. An audience might be greatly disappointed if I breathlessly introduce a guest speaker to them with these words:

NORMAL SIGNIFIER   SLIDING SIGNIFIER

Not only does contextualization transform signifiers by putting them in new relationships with other signifiers, but signifiers themselves refuse to remain stable. They "slide" over the bar separating them from the signified.

They slip along metonymical lines of signification that are actually the natural fault-lines of language. The result is the general instability of meaning. For, relative to the signifier, the signified also slides. (This is one of the features of Lacan's work that separates him from structuralism — that makes him <u>post</u>-structuralist. For structuralism claimed to discover certain universal structures that were the same for everybody, everywhere, always.)

> We are forced, then, to accept the notion of an incessant sliding of the signified under the signifier.

> I THINK, THEREFORE I AM.

> WHAT AM I? I AM A THINKING THING.

> LET'S SEE. HOW WOULD I HAVE SAID THAT WITHOUT LANGUAGE?

In the European intellectual tradition beginning with Descartes, there is the belief in a pre-linguistic selfhood that uses language as an instrument to express its subjectivity.

> I IDENTIFY MYSELF IN LANGUAGE, BUT ONLY BY LOSING MYSELF IN IT LIKE AN OBJECT.

For Lacan, subjectivity is not a <u>thing</u>; rather it is a set of relationships that are activated by entry into a semiological system. There is a paradox here, for Lacan says:

This process of simultaneous discovery and loss starts early. Freud had told of observing an 18-month-old baby who invented a simple game in which he would throw a spool out of his crib, saying "oooh" as he did so, then pull it back into the crib by a string attached to it, saying "aah" as he retrieved it. Freud interpreted "oooh" as the German word "Fort" (away) and "aah" as "Da"

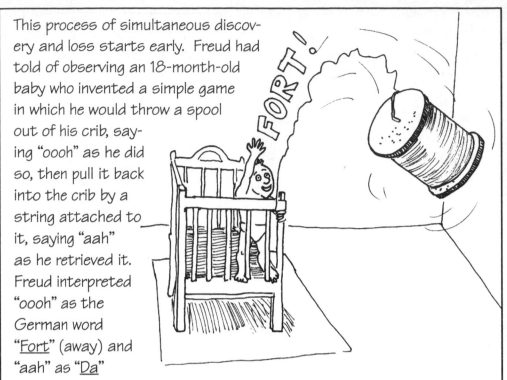

FORT!

(here) and explained that it symbolized to the child the painful disappearance of its mother followed by her comforting return.

Lacan points out that this act of symbolism allows the child to dominate the mystery and terror of the experience of the mother's repeated disappearance, but says that the displacement of the experience onto the symbol also inaugurates the alienation of subjectivity into language that will from then on always be its fate. In fact, the human being is the subject caught and tortured in the web of language. It is this feature of human existence that accounts both for normality and madness.

Freud had claimed that the transition between <u>normality</u> (normality is when one manages to <u>cope</u> with the psychosocial conflicts created by the contradiction between the demands of nature and the demands of culture), <u>neurosis</u> (neurosis is

when that conflict produces "symptoms"— compulsive behavior that seriously interrupts the flow of everyday life), and <u>psychosis</u> (psychosis is madness, where one retreats exclusively into one's symptoms, abandoning the real world) was one of gradation, not a difference in kind. But he admitted that psychoanalysis could not be of help to the psychotic. (Once you go around <u>that</u> bend, it's "Bye-bye, baby.") Lacan, however, wants to demonstrate that psychoanalysis can at least <u>understand</u> the madperson. We see this in his commentary on the case of Daniel Schreber, a prominent German judge who, in 1893, succumbed to mental disease and found himself committed to a clinic for the insane. Ten years later Schreber tried to win his release from the asylum by writing a legal brief called <u>Memoir of My Nervous Illness</u> in which he explains how his body became the site of conflict between two gods, a good one and an inferior one, who had invaded him with voices; how he had survived a cosmic disaster that left him the last human alive; and how magic insects and miraculous birds talked to him during his crisis. (Amazingly, his memoir resulted in

his release.) According to Lacan, Schreber's delirious speech is a speech to which psychoanalysis must listen. And this is possible because it can be shown to be curiously like normal speech.

There are two poles of discourse, whether that be normal discourse or the discourse of delirium: a pole of excess and a pole of deficit. First, there is the <u>language</u> of <u>intuition</u>, which produces a fullness of understanding, but here there is <u>too</u> <u>much</u> meaning— an excess that inhibits communication. At the other extreme there is the empty slogan, the meaningless repetition of words, and emptiness that also precludes communication. The psychotic moves from one pole to the other. The trouble is, so do the rest of us!

Here Lacan retells a joke of Freud's about a chance meeting in a train station of two Polish Jews who distrust each other. "Where are you going?" asks the first. The second says, "To Cracow." The first thinks to himself, "He says he's going to Cracow, but he's saying that so I won't know he's really going to Lemberg. But he <u>knows</u> I'll think that." Then he angrily responds: "You liar, you are going to Cracow!" Once again here are the two linguistic poles of excess and deficit that characterize both "normal" and delirious discourse.

Because this is the form of all discourse. Ideally, the fullness of meaning would be a speech-act that was a testimony and at the same time a self-assertion, such as, "You are my friend." Of course, I want you to respond affirmatively: "Yes, I am your friend." But there is the opposite pole that always threatens the first, namely, the <u>lie</u>. The fact that you can lie causes a perpetual hesitation on my part.

Humans differ from animals in that our relation to what Lacan calls "the Real" is mediated by language. As we have seen, language itself is unstable so there is no guarantee that the mediation will be successful. There are certain basic signifiers, like the one designating the difference between the sexes (what Lacan calls "the phallus"), without which no meaningful human world can be constructed. The basic signifiers are like upholstery buttons that tack down the loose and slippery fabric of signification to specific spots, giving it some stability. If they fail, psychosis happens. In that case no word carries any meaning, or each word carries _all_ meaning, and communication (i.e., intersubjectivity) is impossible. Psychosis is the loss of a grounding signifier and at the same time is the search for its recovery. Lacan says:

IT IS IN MAN'S RELATION TO THE SIGNIFIER THAT THE DRAMA OF MADNESS IS SITUATED.

A psychotic symptom is "a metaphor in which flesh or function is taken as a signifying element." A part of one's body is misrecognized as a part of one's language, and vice-versa. The goal of psychoanalysis, says Lacan, is to restore to the patient "the sovereign freedom displayed by Humpty-Dumpty when he reminds Alice that after all he is the master of the signifier, even if he isn't the master of the signified."

ALICE HAD SAID TO HUMPTY-DUMPTY:

THE QUESTION IS WHETHER YOU *CAN* MAKE WORDS MEAN SO MANY DIFFERENT THINGS

TO WHICH HUMPTY-DUMPTY RESPONDED:

THE QUESTION IS, WHICH IS TO BE MASTER

Madness is just an extreme exaggeration of the dual process of succumbing to the totalitarianism of language and the attempt to resist that totalitarianism by recovering one's freedom.

THE UNCONSCIOUS IS STRUCTURED LIKE A LANGUAGE.

One of Lacan's most famous "one-liners" is:

76

Now, in one sense, this is not a particularly dramatic idea coming from Lacan, since as a structuralist he is committed to the view that <u>everything</u> is structured like a language. But in another sense it is very important because it puts Lacan and Freud on a collision course, for Freud had pretty much tried to biologize the unconscious and at least early in his career had seen psychoanalysis ("the talking cure") as an interim science which someday could be eliminated when more was understood about the human brain. Against the view that the unconscious is an ancient animal remnant, Lacan says:

THE UNCONSCIOUS IS NEITHER PRIMORDIAL NOR INSTINCTUAL.

Furthermore, if the unconscious is like a language, then it is <u>public</u> and not private (for, as Ludwig Wittgenstein [read about him in the upcoming <u>Wittgenstein</u> <u>For</u> <u>Beginners</u>] had said,

THERE IS NO SUCH THING AS A PRIVATE LANGUAGE

In fact, says Lacan, more cryptically,

THE UNCONSCIOUS IS THE DISCOURSE OF THE OTHER.

Language does not simply supply the medium through which private, unconscious thoughts are sometimes expressed; rather language is the <u>site</u> of the unconscious, for biological need is alienated into language as desire (which, by its linguistic nature involves repression) and moves along metonymical and metaphorical chains. (Think of Edgar Allan Poe's line from "The Raven:"

AND THE SILKEN, SAD, UNCERTAIN RUSTLING OF EACH PURPLE CURTAIN, THRILLED ME, FILLED ME WITH FANTASTIC TERRORS NEVER FELT BEFORE

HEY, ANY CHANCE OF GETTING A REFILL HERE?

Here terror of death and desire for death [embodied in "the lost Lenore"] move along the metonymical chain of the "S" sound, and the rhyming of the signifiers, "certain" and "curtain.")

From this it follows that there can be no neutral or "innocent" use of language, no language free from the determination of the unconscious. In fact, the acquisition of language is the inauguration of the unconscious. The unconscious is not some black box into which thoughts and desires are repressed. It finds its home in the very structure of public language. Every linguistic utterance both reveals and conceals. In a sense, everything is before us, not hidden away in a dark room. Slavoj Žižek, the Slovenian Lacanian, makes this point by using the line from an old Marx Brother's movie: Groucho, as a lawyer defending his brother, exclaims:

If appearance and reality are the same, if the unconscious is the discourse of the other, this means that our desires cannot be snatched out of language and fulfilled. Original desires, if we can call them that, are lost in the "chains of the signifiers" and can never be completely recovered. We can only trace the path along which they have traveled.

Sigmund Freud had talked about "unconscious wishes" and tried to show how they are derived from our biology (innate sexual and aggressive drives). Lacan's view is that the place to look for confirmation of Freud's theories is not in biology or neurophysiology but in linguistics. Nevertheless, he does not deny that there is a biological grounding of the human mind. He reserves the word "NEED" to designate biological requirements. Happily, NEEDS can be fulfilled. But DESIRE (being French, Lacan could use the much more slinky word "désir" [=desire] rather than the clunky German word "Wunsch" [=wish] of his Austrian mentor) is much more complicated. Desire is insatiable, being an eternal LACK.

DEMAND IS ALWAYS A DEMAND FOR LOVE...

NEED represents itself in language as DEMAND, but despite appearing to be specific ("Give me that, now!"), demand, by being placed within the semiological system, becomes desire, and as such is ultimately incapable of being satisfied, because,

Lacan says,

GIMME A CANDYBAR NOW!

I JUST GAVE YOU A CANDYBAR

I KNOW, BUT WHAT I REALLY WANTED WAS TOTAL, UNCONDITIONAL LOVE!!

...a love that proves to be impossible once one has entered into the system of signs. (The "union with the mother" is unachievable once the [m]other has been named.)

his takes us to another of Lacan's famous one-liners:

THIS MEANS: To desire is to desire to be desired. But it also means that desire is contageous. We desire what the other desires, and become rivals with the other for the unachievable object of desire. The phrase *also* means that because desire gets caught-up in the metonymical and metaphorical chains of language, desire is public and not private, even if we don't always understand it.

METAPHOR AND DESIRE

What is the process of the alienation of the subject into the chains of the signifier, according to Lacan? He speaks of three "registers" of subjectivity:

the REAL,
the IMAGINARY,
and the SYMBOLIC.

Very little can be said about the REAL. It is the primordial experience of whatever is prior to any attempt to represent it in any system of symbols. It is something like Immanuel Kant's unknowable THING-IN-ITSELF, except that Lacan seems to stress the experience of the thing rather than the way the thing is prior to experience. But once we acquire a language, giving us a system of signs in which to re-present "the real," "the real" is lost to us forever.

Still, we do not enter into language and the SYMBOLIC all at once. We pass into "the IMAGINARY" (and in some ways "the imaginary" coexists with "the symbolic" forever after). The Imaginary register is not just the realm of images or of fantasy, though it is definitely associated with illusion. It is roughly equivalent to everyday experience, but the illusion is that of treating the Symbolic (whose function is to order everyday experience) as if it were real and natural.

Desire inhabits the registers of the Imaginary and the Symbolic. Throughout, the Lacanian slogan, DESIRE IS THE DESIRE OF THE OTHER, is valid. The infant desires the mother, and desires to be desired by her, and desires what she desires. It wants to complete her and fill her lack.

WHAT **DO** WOMEN WANT?

Well, so what is it that the mother desires? (Is this a version of Freud's old question?)

HOW ABOUT A LITTLE RESPECT?

Lacan tells us that the mother desires "the phallus" (not to be confused with the penis— the phallus is rather the SIGN of distinction between the sexes and at the same time of wholeness and the power wholeness would bestow). Therefore the infant desires the phallus and desires to <u>be</u> the phallus. As we saw, this comes down to desiring a perfect (but impossible) union with the mother. But the father, or rather his law (the Law of the Father is a SIGNIFIER, not a person) prevents this. Enter "the Oedipus." But we are moving too fast.

Before the child can enter into the Imaginary and the Symbolic, it must first be able to distinguish between itself and the Other. The moment of this recognition is what Lacan calls THE MIRROR STAGE. Here, between six and eighteen months, the child identifies itself in terms of the image it sees of itself in a mirror. There are, of course, cultures without mirrors, but the stage exists there too. Says Lacan:

THE CHILD WHO STRIKES ANOTHER SAYS THAT HE HAS BEEN STRUCK; THE CHILD WHO SEES ANOTHER FALL CRIES

WAHH

WAHH

This inability to distinguish between subject and object, self and image, is in most respects corrected by the acquistion of language or the entry into "the SYMBOLIC."

Lacan's "symbolic" encompasses language but is more than language. It is the whole set of signs, linguistic and otherwise, that comprises the institutional life of human culture. Entering that world requires the acceptance of systematic prohibition whose main signifier is what Lacan calls THE-NAME-OF-THE-FATHER (which in French allows the pun, the-No-of-the-Father/the-Name-of-the-Father [le-<u>non</u>-<u>du</u>-<u>pere</u>/le-<u>nom</u>-<u>du</u>-<u>pere</u>]). This, then, is the "Oedipal drama," for, as we saw, the main prohibition must be that of the infant's union with its mother.

☞ (Remember, Freud had used the term "Oedipus complex" to designate what for him was a <u>biological</u> propensity— though it only became biological at the moment of the "primordial patricide," when in some Lamarckian way it became incorporated into the human genetic structure— for the child to be erotically attracted to the parent of the opposite sex and hostile to the parent of the same sex. The mythical Oedipus had, after all, killed his father and married his mother.)

Lacan says:

IT IS IN THE NAME OF THE FATHER THAT WE MUST RECOGNIZE THE SUPPORT OF THE SYMBOLIC FUNCTION WHICH, FROM THE DAWN OF HISTORY, HAS IDENTIFIED HIS PERSON WITH THE FIGURE OF THE LAW.

If we add to this Lacan's Saussurean radicalism..

...we see that this SIGNIFIER generates a whole symbolic world of prohibition, repression, alienation and impossible desire, for the sign has "murdered the thing," as one Lacanian has said. It must also be said that this "murder" has produced everything that is great in human culture.

A FINAL ASIDE: **Lacan's replacement of biology with linguistics**
(*e.g.*, his replacement of "the penis" with "the phallus," and his replacement of "the Primal Father" with "the-Name-of-the-Father") has made psychoanalysis a <u>possible</u> science for feminists, having lifted the onerous burden of Freud's "anatomy is destiny," but feminist philosophers and theorists are divided on the result. The critics say that we are liberated from a sexist biologism, but we are still constrained within an equally constrictive and unchanging patriarchal Symbolic Order— that of the Law of the Father.

MICHEL FOUCAULT
(pronounced Me-shéll Foo-có)

ichel Foucault was born in Poitiers, France, in 1926. After graduating from the enormously prestigious Ecole Normal Supériere in Paris, he took teaching jobs in a number of countries, including Sweden, Germany and America. He became a philosophy professor in France at the University of Clermont - Ferrand before being offered a chair at the Collége de France, the nation's most illustrious academy of higher learning. His work ranges over so many fields that to this day, bookstores do not know how to catalogue his writings: philosophy? history? psychology? cultural studies?

Foucault died at fifty eight in 1984 of complications from AIDS.

We have defined STRUCTURALISM in two related ways:

(1) The view that content is reducible to FORM, where the word "form" designates a (usually hidden) structure discoverable behind appearances.

(2) The theory of human reality that applies the principles of Saussure's linguistics to all social phenomena.

The consequence of both (1) <u>and</u> (2) is that there are no ultimate autonomous realities available to human cognition: no gods, no Platonic Forms or Essences, no "atoms," to which everything can be reduced; rather there exist RELATIONSHIPS.

According to this definition, Michel Foucault is a structuralist, especially in his earlier works — this despite his refusal to accept any labels, and despite his suspicions about global theories of totalization (wherein everything is explained in terms of one all-consuming model).

LABELS

NO!

It was this suspicion that led him to reject both psychoanalysis and Marxism, and eventually to reject structuralism itself, as he moved into that nebulous realm called "post-structuralism."

LEAVING THE STRUCTURALISTS' PICNIC

In the ten-year period between 1961 and 1971 in which Foucault produced the most amazing series of books — books that changed the European and American intellectual scene — he tended to deal with language as arbitrary (in the Saussurean sense) and autonomous (in the sense that it is created in its own sphere and was not in need of an extra-linguistic referent in which to ground itself). He was interested both in what Saussure had called _la langue_ (the whole set of phonic and conventional relations that are constitutive of the language into which we are born and which will determine the categories according to which we will think and live), and in what Saussure called _la parôle_ (the individual speech acts in which the various parts of _la langue_ are activated as communicative events) — what Foucault calls DISCOURSE.

PENSE EN FRANÇAIS

VIVE LA FRANCE

BON JOUR

ZOP

"Discourse," however, is certainly not just meaningful noise, nor even just communication. It always has "its links with desire and power," but these links must be masked if desire and power are to manifest themselves in language.

LANGUAGE

Marx had already argued that language was "ideology" which worked in the service of a socio-economic power base that was disguised from language. But Foucault criticizes Marx. Discourse is not reducible to some power base independent of language; rather discourse itself is already "desire and power" in action.

FOUCAULT   MARX

I CONDEMN YOU TO HANG BY THE NECK UNTIL DEAD!

For example, discourse is an inclusionary/exclusionary system whose rules not only determine <u>what</u> can be said, but <u>who</u> can say it. In his works through 1971 (ending with "<u>The Discourse on Language</u>"), Foucault tried to reveal the shadowed side of all forms of discourse purporting to serve "the truth" by demonstrating their duplicitous, deceptive and nefarious nature.

Some of Foucault's books can be seen as histories of various discourses serving different models of "truth"; the discourse of psychiatry (<u>Madness and Civilization</u>, 1962), the discourse of medicine (<u>Birth of the Clinic</u>, 1963), the discourse of social science (<u>The Order of Things</u>, 1966), the discourse of penology (<u>Discipline and Punish</u>, 1975).

But "discourse" itself has a curious and uneven history.

Inspired by the method of the nineteenth - century German philosopher, FRIEDRICH NIETZSCHE, who had also influenced both psychoanalysis and existentialism, Foucault writes what he and Nietzsche called "genealogies" where the discontinuities of history are emphasized, rather than the continuities on which historians usually concentrate.

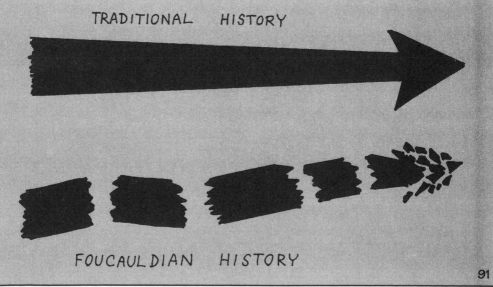

TRADITIONAL   HISTORY

FOUCAULDIAN   HISTORY

In several of his books Foucault describes four such sequences in European (particularly French) history:

(1) the Renaissance (1450-1620),

(2) the Classical Age — sometimes called "the Age of Reason" (most of the seventeenth and eighteenth centuries),

(3) the nineteenth century — sometimes called "the Age of Positivism," and

(4) a future period of which the twentieth century is the beginning. Each of these periods is governed by what Foucault calls an "EPISTEME" (from the Greek word for "knowledge").

By épistème, we mean the total set of relations that unite, at a given period, the discursive practices that give rise to epistemological figures, sciences, and formalized systems.

In other words:

Each society has its régime of truth: that is, the types of discourse which it accepts and makes function as true; the mechanisms and instances which enable one to distinguish true and false statements, the status of those who are charged with saying what counts as true.

To give an obvious example: only in a culture in which the institution of marriage exists can the sentence:

"Xanthippe is married to Socrates," be true, yet the fact that marriage exists is a "discursive fact" (part of a system of discourse). Also of course, there will be those who are empowered to declare marriages valid or invalid.

DADDY, ARE THOSE FROGS MARRIED?

More radically (and perhaps more questionably), only in a culture that has acquiesced to the institution of translating descriptions of natural events into mathematical formulas can a "law" like "F=MA" (force equals mass times acceleration) be true, and only those who have been empowered to do so by yet other discursive practices can state with authority that such laws are true or false.

The rationalist philosophers like Plato and Descartes believed in the innateness and universality of the basic principles of logic: "the principle of identity" (A equals A), "the principle of non-contradiction" (it is not the case that A can be A and not-A at the same time), and "the principle of the excluded middle" (either A or not-A). Foucault shows that each épistème chooses how to apply these principles, chooses what will be called "THE SAME" (A) and "DIFFERENCE" (not-A). That is, it chooses how to define a "We" and how to exclude an "Other."

WE

93

The Order Of Things (1966) can be viewed as a "history of the same," while Madness and Civilization (1961), The Birth of the Clinic (1963), Discipline and Punish (1975), and the three volumes of The History of Sexuality (1976-84), are histories of what is considered the "abnormal." The connection between the two histories is structural and dialectical, just as in Saussure's linguistics. An official "We" can be established only as a function of the official designation of Otherness.

We will use Madness and Civilization as our primary example of Foucault's work, both because of its accessibility, and its closeness to Foucault's structuralist roots.

Despite its subtitle, A History of Insanity in the Age of Reason, in the preface Foucault tells his readers that his book is a history of "that other form of madness" by which "men confine their neighbors" to asylums and designate them as "mentally ill." The book is about the silence that the language of psychiatry has imposed on the language of madness.

It was not always so. Once there was a dialogue between reason and unreason, a "stammering of imperfect words without fixed syntax." Foucault asks us to return to an historical moment before the separation of reason and unreason, when they were still experienced as an undifferentiated unity he tells us:

THE GREEK *Logos* HAD NO CONTRARY

(<u>Logos</u> is the Greek term for "Reason," and also for "Word," as in the first sentence of the Book of John in the Bible: "In the beginning was the Logos, and the Logos was with God, and the Logos was God.") Socrates, in fact, had used the phrase "divine madness" to designate both the inspiration of the poets and that of the oracles of the gods in the temple. (Some of these spokespersons for the gods were apparently epileptics, and one of them had declared Socrates to be the wisest man in Greece). The Greeks communed with the madness in their soul both by listening to its murmur in themselves—

ME? THE WISEST MAN IN GREECE? IMPOSSIBLE. I KNOW NOTHING.

BUT THEN AGAIN, I <u>KNOW</u> THAT I KNOW NOTHING, WHICH IS MORE THAN ANYBODY ELSE KNOWS...

(Socrates had a "daemon" within to which he always deferred)— and to its voice in others (to the sometimes unintelligible babbling of the oracles, and to the wailing and the shrieking of the chorus in the tragedies).

So originally [the later "post-structuralist" Foucault would abandon all attempts to return to "originals" or to "pure experiences"], reason and unreason were not isolated from each other... because there was still a (stammered) discourse between them.

REASON

UNREASON

That was before

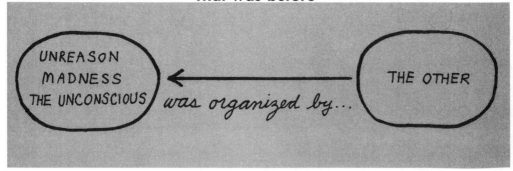

UNREASON
MADNESS
THE UNCONSCIOUS · *was organized by...* · THE OTHER

After Foucault's preface to <u>Madness and Civilization</u>, the Greeks are not mentioned again. His "history of madness" actually begins in the last days of the medieval world. The first chapter called "Stultifera Navis" ("The Ship of Fools"), begins with this line:

> AT THE END OF THE MIDDLE AGES, LEPROSY DISAPPEARED FROM THE WESTERN WORLD

During the medieval period the leper had been excluded, but his physical exclusion was a form of <u>sacred inclusion</u>. The leper was a religious signifier. He signified a divine meaning. Jesus had conferred with the lepers; he had cured them and made their presence part of a religious morality play.

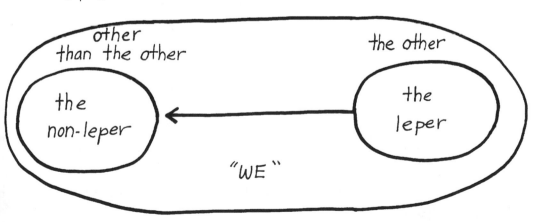

The leper disappeared, but the exclusionary/ inclusionary structure remained, and the leper's "slot" was filled by "the fool." Suddenly "the ship of fools" appears and "invades the most familiar landscapes." (The mad were placed on boats that sailed up and down the rivers of Europe. Food would be taken to the piers by the citizens when the boats passed through.) Why this new fascination with madness?

BECAUSE IT SYMBOLIZED A GREAT DISQUIET, SUDDENLY DAWNING ON THE HORIZON OF EUROPEAN CULTURE AT THE END OF THE MIDDLE AGES. IT SIGNIFIED THE DIZZYING UNREASON OF THE WORLD.

Previously the image of death had terrified the people of the Middle Ages. Now "the mockery of madness replaces death." Yet, as in the case of lepers, the madman's exclusion is also an inclusion. There is still a "We," because there is still communication.

The mad person's image is a sign. It too signifies a religious meaning. (The paintings of Hieronymus Bosch with their lunatic figures and mad landscapes are <u>religious</u> paintings.) The image of insanity is apocalyptic. It invokes the end of the world. "Madness fascinates because it is knowledge."

Albrecht Dürer

FREED FROM WISDOM AND FROM THE TEACHING THAT ORGANIZED IT, THE IMAGE BEGINS TO GRAVITATE AROUND ITS OWN MADNESS.

This wisdom of fools foretells the reign of Satan and the end of the world. But the message is frenzied and chaotic. People no longer understand the old Gothic symbolism.

THAT IS, THE SIGNIFIER GOES BERSERK.

The theme of lunacy will eventually stabilize, but will last throughout the Renaissance. One of the most popular books of the period will be Erasmus's <u>In Praise of Folly</u>. And at the end of the era, some of the greatest artistic works are about madness. The folly of Cervantes' <u>Don Quixote</u> is both "madness by romantic identification" and "madness of vain presumption."

The delirium of Shakespeare's Lady Macbeth is "the madness of just punishment," while the insanity of Ophelia in Hamlet and the bittersweet madness of his King Lear is "the madness of desperate passion." Even though this madness let loose during the Renaissance is more secular than religious, it is still connected with the moral discourse between reason and unreason established at the end of the medieval world. But it is the last moment of this specific discourse.

A new épistème is about to burst forth, and in the seventeenth century madness will cease to be an "eschatological figure" (i.e. , a figure announcing the end of the world). The voyage of the "ship of fools" will end, the ship moored and made fast, "no longer a ship but a hospital."

It will be the age of "The Great Confinement."

But it was not just "the insane" who would be hospitalized, but also the poor, the unemployed, the criminal, and young men who squandered their fortunes. This is an odd grouping from our point of view, but to the classical age it was a "logical" one.

(We have a hard time seeing this, just as Lévi-Strauss's Nambikwara Indian hosts had a hard time seeing that a full-grown male Blue Whale [the largest creature ever to have lived on earth] and a mole [the smallest mammal in South America] were THE SAME simply because both had nipples [!], and as Lévi-Strauss would have a hard time seeing that "palm leaves," "toads," and "shoulders" are THE SAME because they all belong to the class of objects that are warm and dry on top, and dark and damp underneath . . .)

What is it that the classical age, in its "clearly articulated perception" <u>sees</u> as the common denominator in this strange group? SLOTH, INDOLENCE and IDLENESS. This is not an <u>economic</u> judgment (Marx was wrong about that), but a <u>moral</u> judgment derived from the new épistème's work ethic.

The cure for madness (and all these other disabilities) was WORK. This moral and juridical imposition of ORDER and REASON had nothing to do with medicine.

YOU MEAN IT WASN'T JUST PROTESTANTS WHO WANTED TO WORK?

MAX WEBER

TODAY'S EXHIBIT: LIONS, TIGERS AND BEARS, AND LUNATICS

Despite lumping the mad together with indigents and criminals into hospitals, the insane were selected out to be exhibited. Before, they had been seen on the highways and byways and rivers of Europe; now they were seen behind bars, like animals.

In fact, the seventeenth and eighteenth century saw madness as a return to animality. But oddly enough, in European history up to this point, animals were not seen as part of nature, they were seen as anti-nature.

THE HOSPITAL OF BETHLEHEM IN LONDON EXHIBITED LUNATICS FOR A PENNY.

NATURE (with its wise ways) — ANTI-NATURE
-BEASTS
-THE MAD

Think of the poet William Blake's beastly tiger:

Tiger! Tiger! burning bright
In the forests of the night
What immortal hand or eye
Could frame thy fearful symmetry?
What the hammer? What the chain?
In what furnace was thy brain?
What the anvil? What dread grasp
Dare its deadly terrors clasp?

But the madman, though now confined and silenced, is still a sign — a sign of how close to animality the Fall of Man has brought humanity. Despite its muted words, there is still a discourse between unreason and reason, as the lunatic reminds us of the possibility of a monstrous, frenzied freedom.

Today we see insanity as a form of DETERMINISM. (The madwoman is not guilty, for she cannot do otherwise than what she does. She is unfree.)

But the Age of Reason, saw madness as a terrifying, unchained, raging, freedom. Furthermore, that age did not see the mad as sick. In fact, their madness prevents them from being sick. In the Age Of Reason madness was associated not only with animality, but with PASSION. Passion did not <u>cause</u> madness, but the <u>possibility</u> of madness. One's own passion was a sign of the possibility of madness, hence the madness of the other was the possibility of one's own madness. Descartes had shown that soul and body were united, but the unity was fragile, and where the two overlapped was passion.

105

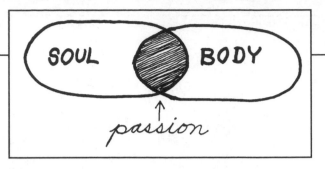

Madness, if it set in, could destroy both soul and body. Passions discharged themselves in terms of IMAGES. Madness itself is not imagination, but madness surrenders itself to the immediacy of the image. (You imagine that you are made of glass [an image made famous by both Cervantes and Descartes], or you imagine that you are dead. Everyone imagines such things. This is not madness. Madness is giving over to the image — acting on it.) Madness connects the image to a DISCOURSE. The 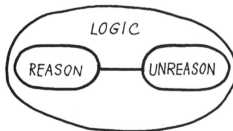 madman "organizes the image around a segment of a language." He tells himself, "I am made of glass." Madness is not just in the IMAGE or the LANGUAGE around which the image is organized; it lies in drawing logical deductions from this unity — in thinking, "therefore I am fragile and may not come in contact with any other person. I must remain motionless."

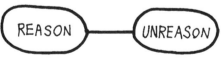

Madness is reason's other,...

...but their logic is the same.

The mad person makes LOGICAL deductions. The logic of madness is THE SAME as the logic of the logicians.

Indeed, according to the classical conception,

...AT THE HEART OF MADNESS, AT THE CORE OF SO MANY ERRORS... WE DISCOVER FINALLY, THE HIDDEN PERFECTION OF A LANGUAGE... THE ULTIMATE LANGUAGE OF MADNESS IS THAT OF REASON, BUT THE LANGUAGE OF REASON ENVELOPED IN THE PRESTIGE OF THE IMAGE.

(Consider Descartes' "I THINK THEREFORE I AM." A perfect sentence, pure logic found at the very heart of his solipsistic delirium, of his paranoid method of doubt.)

EVIL DEMONS
ROBOTS THAT LOOK LIKE HUMANS
DREAMS
ILLUSIONS
I THINK, THEREFORE I AM

MATTERS OF WAR ARE MORE SUBJECT THAN MOST TO CONTINUAL CHANGE. A SORCERER HAS TURNED THOSE GIANTS INTO WINDMILLS, TO CHEAT ME OF THE GLORY OF CONQUERING THEM, BUT IN THE END HIS BLACK ARTS SHALL AVAIL HIM LITTLE AGAINST THE GOODNESS OF MY SWORD.

(Think of the exquisite logic of Don Quixote explaining his "defeat" by the windmills that he's mistaken for giants.)

THERE'S NOTHING LIKE EATING HAY WHEN YOU'RE FAINT.

I SHOULD THINK SMELLING-SALTS WOULD BE BETTER

I DIDN'T SAY THERE WAS NOTHING BETTER. I SAID THERE WAS NOTHING LIKE IT.

(Or, jumping ahead a few hundred years, think of the hyper-logic of the characters in Lewis Carroll's "Wonderland" and "Looking - Glass Land" — for example, when the king's messenger faints, the king suggests they feed him hay.)

But this pure logic is applied to a system of <u>false</u> <u>propositions</u> in the general syntax of a dream.

DREAMS AND MADNESS, THEN, APPEARED TO BE OF THE SAME SUBSTANCE.

(Descartes had said that dreams are a form of temporary insanity, and because he thought we dream all night [otherwise we would stop thinking, and therefore stop existing], he believed we spend about one-third of our lives insane.)

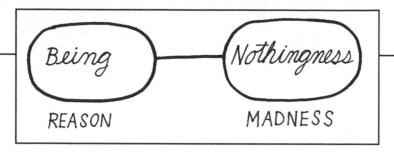

REASON   **MADNESS**

As such, madness is a form of ERROR. These mad dream images represent NOTHING; they are the culmination of the void — nothingness.

Madness ceases to be the sign of another world. It is the manifestation of non-being. If you look too long into the sun, then look away, there is a black spot — a nothingness — in the middle of your visual field. You have been dazzled by the sun. "Dazzlement is night in broad daylight. Madness is reason dazzled."

CONFINEMENT OF THE MAD IS "AN OPERATION TO ANNIHILATE NOTHINGNESS."

I BAPTIZE THEE...

As the eighteenth century progresses, <u>error</u> became <u>fault</u>. "Non-being" becomes the natural punishment of a <u>moral</u> <u>evil</u> which is associated with "pure subjectivity" — that is, to be mad is to break with the universal objective moral order. One of the treatments of madness in this century is IMMERSION in water. Foucault quotes from an account of contemporary "therapy": "The sufferer came down the corridors to the ground floor, and arrived in a square vaulted room, in which a pool had been constructed; he was pushed over backward into the water."

Immersion represents both a religious conversion and a return to nature. In the second half of the eighteenth century (under the influence of Rousseau) a return to nature is seen as capable of curing madness, for nature "has the power of freeing man from his freedom."

SUCH VIOLENCE PROMISED THE REBIRTH OF A BAPTISM.

The classical period had seen a strange similarity between Reason (after which the "Age" had named itself) and Unreason. Madness was like "a darkened mirror" in which sanity was reflected and caricatured.

This caricature of Reason produced some amusement, but "fear and anxiety were not far off." The fear was, that the place where evil was confined — the asylum — was itself a birthplace of evil, a rotten sinkhole from which evil could spread. The <u>air</u> of the asylum was believed to be tainted.

THESE ARE THOUGHTS HALFWAY BETWEEN MEDICINE AND MORALITY.

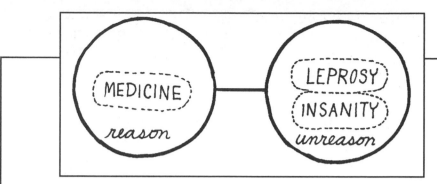

Now "the circle was closed." The original exclusion was the exclusion of the ill (lepers). Once again it is the ill who are excluded. But it is <u>fantasy</u> which discovers/creates this illness, not medicine.

Even though there is a return to an earlier point, something NEW is being invented, because at the end of the eighteenth century, FEAR and desire merge to create something novel. (In the next generation, the Danish philosopher, Søren Kierkegaard, would define DREAD as a fear of what one desires, and a desire of what one fears.) What morality wants to exorcise, desire wishes to experience.

What is being invented about the time of the French Revolution is madness as a contagious dialogue between LOVE and DEATH, namely, SADISM and MASOCHISM are being constructed.

And along with it, a new kind of madness is being created.

fears/desires
(i.e., "dreads")

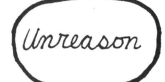

One of the main morals of Foucault's story is beginning to unfold. UNREASON is ATEMPORAL, MADNESS IS HISTORICAL. There is an eternal recurrence of the threat of unreason, but the threat of madness is a <u>modern</u> threat. "Madness" is an historical artifact. Naming the illness, and confining it, is modernity's way of:

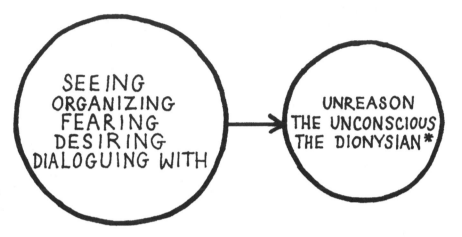

SEEING
ORGANIZING
FEARING
DESIRING
DIALOGUING WITH

→

UNREASON
THE UNCONSCIOUS
THE DIONYSIAN*

*(Nietzsche's name for the frenzied, ecstatic chaos to be found in the heart of all humans except those who have already been defeated by civilization.)

In the Renaissance, madness was on the horizon of Nature. It represented a BREAK with NATURE. It was a sign with a moral message reminding us of The Fall, and the expulsion from the Garden of Eden. In the second half of the eighteenth century, madness is on the horizon of <u>civilization</u>.

Civilization itself is a "break with the immediate" (i.e., with that which is given to us directly by Nature) and as such, CIVILIZATION (<u>not</u> animality, <u>not</u> sin) is the pre-condition of madness — civilization, with its advantages, and its sadomasochistic possibilities.

According to the mythology of the history of psychiatry, two heroes, Samuel Tuke in England, and Phillipe Pinel in France, liberated the mad from their chains and separated them from the slothful, approaching their mental illness with compassion and scientific rigor. Foucault sees it otherwise. The poor were liberated from confinement not for humanitarian reasons, but because their manpower was needed by the new industrialism. Those left behind, the truly mad, will now be given ASYLUM — in every sense of the word. In these new asylums the mad will be freed from the onus of <u>moral</u> guilt, but they must be made aware that they are GUILTY OF BEING MAD. It is explained to the insane that they are being treated kindly (no chains, no brutality) and they must promise to restrain themselves. The madman was forced to see himself as mad, and to hold himself responsible for being so. In fact, "madness no longer exists except as seen."

Tuke believes the mad have a need for self-esteem, and this explanation is found in WORK (the bourgeois solution for all ills). The mad are rewarded with "tea parties," where the guests dress in their best clothes and observe themselves imitating all the rules of social life. Specifically, the mad imitate the rules of FAMILY life.

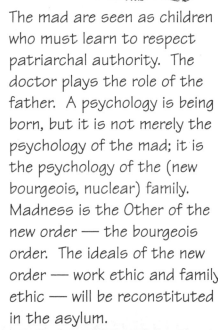

The mad are seen as children who must learn to respect patriarchal authority. The doctor plays the role of the father. A psychology is being born, but it is not merely the psychology of the mad; it is the psychology of the (new bourgeois, nuclear) family. Madness is the Other of the new order — the bourgeois order. The ideals of the new order — work ethic and family ethic — will be reconstituted in the asylum.

work family → work family

REASON   UNREASON

No surprise that eventually psychoanalysis would analyze madness in terms of "family values" — Oedipus complex, incest, patricide. In fact, to his credit,

FREUD RESTORED THE POSSIBILITY OF A DIALOGUE WITH UNREASON.

And he was able to unravel some of the forms madness has taken on (namely, those forms that were the mockery of the family structure). Nevertheless, psycho-analysis "remains a stranger" to the larger enterprise of Unreason.

THE DIONYSIAN SCREAM

It seems that for Foucault, in Madness and Civilization, Unreason (that is, the ahistorical unconscious, the dionysian scream of frenzy and ecstasy in the soul of human beings) is some-thing highly valuable, and as the ancient Greeks knew, the health of the human soul requires its expression and the absorption of its message. (A very Nietzschean theme — roughly the thesis of Nietzsche's first book, The Birth of Tragedy, 1872.)

Furthermore, it seems that throughout Western history the very fear of Unreason has resulted in military-like operations designed to isolate, keep watch over, and manage the anti-social nature of Unreason, leading to the confinement of those blessed with too much of its fearful freedom, silencing the voice of "madness, insanity, lunacy."

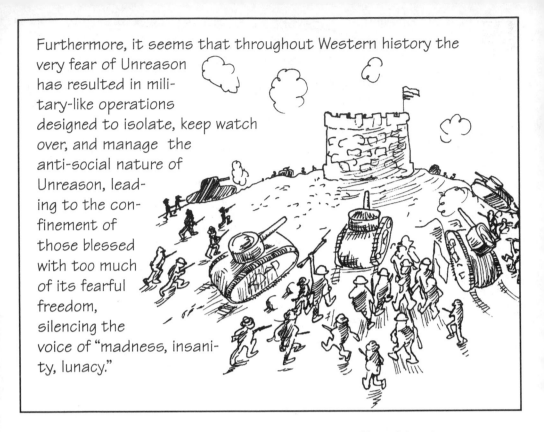

TWAS BRILLIG AND THE SLITHY TOVES DID GYRE AND GIMBLE IN THE WABE

LET'S TALK ABOUT IT.

Freud is given some credit for entering into a one-on-one dialogue with Unreason, but because this occurs squarely within the confines of a new form of totalitarian bourgeois familial authority, this "liberation" of the voice of Unreason creates and constricts the very voice with which it discourses. Hence finally Freud's name too must be added to those of Pinel and Tuke as false Messiahs of Unreason.

What, then, has been the fate of Unreason to the extent that it has resisted psychiatric organization?

SINCE THE END OF THE EIGHTEENTH CENTURY, THE LIFE OF UNREASON NO LONGER MANIFESTS ITSELF EXCEPT IN THE LIGHTENING-FLASH OF WORKS SUCH AS THOSE OF HÖLDERLIN, OR NERVAL, OF NIETZSCHE, OR OF ARTAUD.

These poets and philosophers eventually did slip too deeply into "their dark freedom." Even though art and madness are profoundly entwined, art after all is <u>not</u> madness. Still, art <u>is</u> Unreason. Foucault wants art, not madness.

MADNESS IS PRECISELY THE ABSENCE OF THE WORK OF ART

NIETZSCHE'S LAST CRY, PROCLAIMING HIMSELF BOTH CHRIST AND DIONYSOS, IS THE VERY ANNIHILATION OF THE WORK OF ART

So, even though "madness" is a socio-historical product created by each épistème as its inverted mirror-image mocking the historical version of "Reason" that created it, Foucault admits that there is a place where there is too much Unreason. When Nietzsche, Van Gogh, Hölderin and Artaud really do go mad, they slip from that auspicious place where Being and Nothingness hold a profound dialogue, into the dark silence of total nothingness.

PURE NOTHINGNESS

THE SAUSSUREAN BOX

From about 1973 forward, Foucault and others who had been called Structuralists came to think of the Saussurean linguistic model (according to which all events were versions of discourse) as suffering from certain limitations. Though Foucault did not veer from his view that discursive acts were deployments of power, he needed an extra-linguistic model of power. In <u>Discipline and Punish</u> (1975), social reality could no longer be reduced to linguistic categories. Furthermore, Foucault's idea of power changed.

YOU *WILL* MAKE THE TRAIN RUN ON TIME!

Earlier, in <u>Madness and Civilization</u> and in <u>The Birth of The Clinic</u>, the exercise of power was always repressive (one person or a group of people making another group of people do things they don't want to do).

But external violence has become internal violence. Power is like a web extending its lines everywhere in a crisscrossing pattern. Now power must be understood in a context of background institutions, practices and discourses which both create power and are created by power. Rather than being merely constraining or punitive, this new power is <u>productive</u>. As power mutates in different épistèmes, it generates new kinds of desires and new kinds of <u>subjects</u>; in fact, power is not really wielded by individuals at all, rather it is an organization of relationships of individuals and institutions in which everyone is involved. Everyone and no one is a <u>victim</u> of power.

119

But don't misunderstand this.

There is certainly no more freedom in this new model of power
that there was on the
Saussurean model. Worse,
it is unclear how there
could be any form of resis-
tance to power here, where
everything is power. (One
of the main criticisms of
Foucault's later work is
that it allows for no
political agenda against power
or its abuse. Every act is a
version of every other act.)

WORKERS OF THE WORLD, UNITE!!

AGAINST WHAT?

SOAP

Foucault's final set of impressive works was <u>The History of Sexuality</u>.
In these books, Foucault attacks the traditional liberal view that
power <u>represses</u> sexuality. To the contrary, power <u>produces</u> sexuality.

SEX SEX SEX

SEX SEX SEX

In fact, far from being
supressed, sexuality in the
Victorian period was
obsessively discussed. The
Victorians participated in
the same myth heard often
today — that there is a
true "human nature" which
needs to be expressed, and
that our sexuality is an
important part of that
nature.

But according to Foucault, above and beyond the actual facts of our biology, "sexuality" is a new historical product of a system of surveillance, control, and self-expression. It is the very discussion of our sexuality that creates our sexuality. During the medieval period, sex was about the body, and in the confessionals people confessed things they did with their bodies. But during the Reformation and Counter-Reformation (sixteenth and seventeenth centuries) the concern was not just about bodily activities, but about intentions. Sexuality was becoming a <u>psychological</u> fact. We confess to the priests, but we begin to need experts to put our sexuality (hence our need for self-fulfillment) into speech. This generates a strategy of power that produces not only self-scrutiny, but psychiatrists, psychologists, psychoanalysts and social workers, all of whom produce a discourse of power that is meant to liberate a sexuality which in fact is only <u>invented</u> by the discourses and practices that are meant to liberate it. The constraints imposed by power are no longer external, but internal, being part of the discursive rules that generate the facts.

MEDIEVAL PERIOD

COUNTER-REFORMATION

By the time of his death in 1984, Foucault had completed only three of the projected five volumes of his <u>The History of Sexuality</u>. Though unfinished, his revolutionary thoughts on this topic have continued to exert tremendous influence wherever sex is thought about.

Early on, one of Foucault's main works, <u>Madness and Civilization</u>, was soundly criticized by a young French philosopher named Jacques Derrida, who took Foucault to task for claiming to write a history of madness in which he spoke on behalf of the mad from a standpoint outside madness. Foucault responded with great disdain, pooh-poohing as mere word games the whole of Derrida's newly famous post-structuralist philosophy called "deconstruction."

Let's end our romp across the structuralist and post-structuralist landscape by looking at these "word games" of Jacques Derrida.

JACQUES
DERRIDA
(B. 1930)
(pronounced "JOCK DARE-EE-DÁ)

acques Derrida was born in a suburb of Algiers in North Africa in 1930 to a middle-class Jewish family. After earning his baccalaureate degree, as a nineteen-year-old student, he went to France and enrolled in philosophy courses at the École Normale. He was early influenced by the existentialism of Jean-Paul Sartre and Albert Camus, though he soon became critical of this philosophy. He dropped out of the university, having lost interest in the topic of his own doctoral dissertation.

It wasn't until 1980 that he actually took his examination. By then he had already published numerous books and articles that had earned him a reputation as an important post-structuralist thinker, particularly in America, where in 1966 he had made a big splash at Johns Hopkins University. The next year, three major works were published and his fame was also established in his native France. He now teaches at the International College of Philosophy in Paris and at the University of California at Irvine.

Of Grammatology (1967) is Derrida's main early work. Its key topic is one that at first glance would not seem very important to the uninitiated reader. It is Derrida's discovery of a prejudice among linguists, anthropologists and philosophers against WRITING as opposed to SPEECH.

BIG DEAL!

OF GRAMMATOLOGY

But, according to Derrida, this prejudice is significant because it dominates Western thinking from its inception — a kind of thinking that Derrida calls "LOGOCENTRIC" — and is indicative of an all-pervasive metaphysical bias that is in urgent need of "DECONSTRUCTION." (More on the two key terms in a minute.)

LOGOCENTRIC? DECONSTRUCTION? Oh MAN! Wasn't it enough with diachronic and synchronic and mytheme and épistème and metonymy and semiotics? NOW THIS!

STRUCTURALISM & POST-STRUCTURALISM FOR BEGINNERS

This bias can be traced at least as far back in the tradition as Socrates (469 - 399 BC) who refused to write down any of his thoughts on the grounds that true philosophy had to be a living, conversational exchange of ideas between two or more people, and that the written record of this exchange would be an empty, fossilized skeleton.

Socrates' student, Plato (427-347 BC), argued in favor of his teacher's views by writing a dialogue — the Phaedrus — recording Socrates' attack on writing.

BLAH BLAH BLAH

BLAH BLAH BLAH

ARE WE DOING PHILOSOPHY YET?

SOCRATES SAYS THAT THE WRITTEN WORD IS UNTRUTHFUL. IT'S ALL WRITTEN OUT RIGHT HERE.

(Derrida does not miss the irony of all this!)

Plato's student, Aristotle (384-322 BC), while rejecting Socrates' horror of the written word, agreed that the spoken word has priority over the written. In his book On Interpretation, Aristotle holds the view that thoughts in the mind are those things with which we are in direct contact, and that the spoken word is a sign of those ideas, and that the written word is merely a sign of a sign. Therefore, the written word is at the greatest remove from the immediate truth.

The same prejudice comes into the Christian tradition from St. Paul, who **writes**:

THE LETTER KILLETH BUT THE SPIRIT GIVETH LIFE

In the modern period, Derrida finds the same bias throughout the work of the great Swiss philosopher Jean-Jacques Rousseau (1712-1778), whose ideas were influential during the French Revolution.

ROUSSEAU CONDEMNS WRITING AS A DESTRUCTION OF PRESENCE AND AS A DISEASE OF SPEECH.

Rousseau believes that a true human community exists only where direct, undeceptive communication exists, and like Socrates, he believes this can only happen in a living exchange of ideas. (His conception of democracy was based on his memory of the town meetings of the small Swiss cantons.) But writing helps destroy the organic community and its face-to-face encounters. Writing replaces it with vast networks of mass-communication and with the increasing abuse of power and loss of justice that follows. Those who control writing are the priests and the law-givers, so writing becomes the primary instrument of social control.

Even the hero of the first part of our book, Ferdinand de Saussure, proves to have incorporated this "logocentric" prejudice into his linguistic theory.

> YOU MEAN EVEN I AM GOING TO GET DECONSTRUCTED?

This is because Saussure had <u>written</u> about the dangers of taking writing too seriously.

> ALL I SAID WAS: "WRITING VEILS THE APPEARANCE OF LANGUAGE; IT IS NOT A GUISE FOR LANGUAGE BUT A DISGUISE."

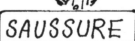

SAUSSURE

Derrida also finds that Claude Lévi-Strauss exhibits the same bias. In <u>Tristes Tropiques</u>, Lévi-Strauss confesses his feelings of guilt because of introducing writing into the innocent lives of the Nambikwara tribe he studied in the Amazon Basin.

> OH! THE GUILT!

Now, according to Derrida, this bias is not just "phonocentrism" — the privileging of spoken sound over script — it is **LOGOCENTRISM**. ("Logos" meant "word" in ancient Greek, and it is also the term from which we get our word "logic," as well as "...logy" ["the theory of," or "the study of," as in "biology," the study of life]. So it is the WORD infused by the CONCEPT. It was translated into Latin as "ratio" or REASON.) Logocentrism, in prioritizing the spoken word over the written word, is also privileging an original meaning over its supposed repetition, just as it privileges a present meaning over an abstract one, an origin over a copy. This belief system constitutes a whole metaphysics, and a very Platonic one at that. (Recall that, for Plato, the philosopher's job was the transcending of the physical world, which is merely a world of copies, in order to return to and grasp an original world of eternal [always present] Truth.)

So Derrida's attack on the traditional prioritizing of speech over writing is really an attack on the metaphysics of absolute presence and of absolute origins.

How does Derrida engage in this attack? He certainly does not do it by claiming absurdly that, historically, <u>first</u> there was writing, <u>then</u> there was speech.

He doesn't even deny Saussure's right to downplay writing as a practical feature of linguistics.

Then on what level <u>is</u> he questioning it? On a <u>logical</u> level. He does this by showing that the very nature of writing (in terms of those of its features to which its detractors have objected) is present <u>both</u> in speech and writing. He shows that speech and writing have the same essential features—that is—there is no CONCEPT of writing that essentially distinguishes it from speaking. Both are SIGNS (in the Saussurean sense). Both depend on their REPEATABILITY for their usefulness. Both are RELATIONAL (also in Saussure's sense — they are what the others are not), which means that in the case of both speech and writing there is never an ORIGINAL PRESENCE; there is in both cases a PARTIAL PRESENCE and a PARTIAL ABSENCE. This is true, for instance, whether I <u>think</u>, <u>say</u> or <u>write</u> the words "dog", "philosophy", or my own name.

Derrida continues his attack on those who attack writing not only by showing that all those attacks are delivered in <u>writing</u> (St. Paul writes a letter in letters saying that the letter killeth), but also by showing that those detractors of writing employ the figures of writing as key parts of their arguments. (Plato illustrates his theory by using metaphors of deciphering codes and of engraving; Saussure explains his theory of phonetics by comparing it to writing.) And the attacks on writing often hypocritically disguise concerns other than merely philosophical anxieties about language.

TAKE THIS!

WE NEED TO TALK

READ MY BOOK

(Rousseau claims that only in direct human encounters can one reveal one's true thoughts and feelings, yet he is personally incapable of revealing himself in such face-to-face encounters, so he has recourse to the written word to produce a confessional revelation of his true thoughts.)

Some of his private thoughts have to do with the evils of masturbation, which Rousseau associates with writing, because writing is <u>supplementary</u> to the <u>real</u> act of speaking, and masturbation is supplemenatry to <u>real</u> sex. So Rousseau's attack on writing is really a moral treatise based on his fear of masturbation.

Similarly, Derrida gives a careful reading of Lévi-Strauss's "The Writing Lesson" in <u>Tristes Tropiques</u> and shows that "writing" already existed among the Nambikwara long before the arrival of the guilty anthropologist.

The whole of Nambikwara culture is already based on signs — with all of the attendant Saussurean implications — and therefore it already has its own hierarchy of rank and its manipulation of power. In fact, like Barthes, Derrida uses this insight to attack the whole "nature" versus "culture" distinction in the West (which is already part of the metaphysics of presence and origins). What we mean by "nature" is part of a semiological system.

Derrida invents a name for this conglomeration of semiotic features common both to speech and writing and so essential to each that it absorbs their differences. He calls it ARCHE-WRITING (<u>arche-écriture</u> in French). "Arche-writing" is the system of cultural signs that will always pre-exist — that is, be presupposed by — both speech and writing in their normal "narrow" definitions. Derrida's "grammatology" is a study of this "arche-writing". But Derrida does not claim that he can find a position outside of arch-writing where he can stand on higher, more neutral ground and look objectively back in on it.

To write about writing is always to write from the inside, and there-fore, in a sense, no one can ever escape from logocentrism, but we can at least reveal what is in fact obscured and repressed by that metaphysics.

male	/	female
light	/	dark
right	/	left
philosophy	/	fiction
science	/	myth
presence	/	absence
high	/	low
cooked	/	raw

THESE ARE SUPERIOR!

As we just saw, from his "deconstruction" of the distinction between speech and writing, Derrida derives the further "deconstruction" of the nature/ culture opposition that was so dear to Rousseau and to Lévi-Strauss. In fact, it will be recalled that much of Lévi-Strauss' structuralism was an attempt to depict the human mind as busy constructing categories of binary opposites like the nature/culture one: for example, raw/cooked, male/female, light/dark, high/low, left/right, life/death. But according to Derrida, these turn out to be not only key categories of structuralism, but of "logocentric" dis-course itself. Furthermore, logocentric reasoning tends to privilege one of the two poles of these "necessary" binary opposites.

Derrida tries to show that, in all cases, the prioritizing of one pole over the other displays mere cultural manipulations of power, and to show that, under deconstructive scrutiny, these oppositions break down and collapse into each other. In what will surely be bad news for many, even the distinction between structure and lack of structure (chaos?) seems to break down under Derrida's gaze.

Two of the major binary oppositions done away with by Derrida are those of presence/absence, and origin/supplement. Let us return to the idea of the "metaphysics of presence" and the search for absolute origins. This metaphysics manifests itself in many guises. As we saw, one was Plato's attempt to trace language and meaning back to some absolute "Form" or essence which would be revealed by a special kind of philosophical quest as being an absolute, certain, unmoving, unchanging Truth. Another would be the medieval search for God, whose necessary and absolute existence would ground all the uncertainties and contingencies of finite existence. Another would be Descartes' search for the self — his, "I think therefore I am" — as the absolute foundation of all thought. Another would be Rousseau's attempt to return to nature. Yet another would be the belief in the absolute existence of the present moment as opposed to the lost past and the yet-to-arrive future (a favorite idea of the phenomenologists and existentialists). All of these philosophical notions assume that thought and language can arrive at something fully present, a fullness of being or an absolute origin.

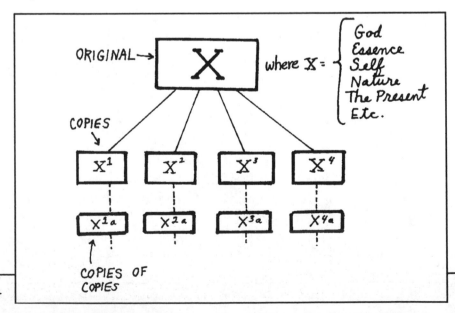

I THINK, **THERE**FORE I AM

In fact, either a study of language or a careful attention to actual experience refutes these fraudulent hopes. Every moment of the present is loaded with a no-longer extant past and is at the same time pregnant with a future. Experience itself is a combination of a presence and absence.

Non-being is experienced as a part of being. The same discovery is made when we turn to language and meaning. Language is temporal. Every speech-act in the present takes place through time and refers to past and present.

And as Saussure had pointed out, every sign is incomplete without all the other signs. Meaning is not found at any one place in language; it is diffused throughout the whole system of signs. Each sign has traces of all other signs, and they cannot be kept out even though they are not really "there".

NOTHING IS ANYWHERE EVER SIMPLY PRESENT OR ABSENT

We are trapped in what Derrida calls "the logic of supplementarity."

According to structural linguistics, meaning is possible only because there is a DIFFERENCE among signs. Add to this Derrida's claim that meaning is never present but is always DEFERRED. Derrida invents a new French word to cover these two curious facts: DIFFÉRANCE (as opposed to the normal French word, différence, pronounced the same way). This amounts to an intentional radicalization of Saussure's theory of linguistics, but one which only takes advantage of logical features of Saussure's discoveries that were already there, but features that he failed to notice, or even suppressed, for the logic of "différance" means that no theory of language can ever succeed as a science, since it must always work within a language and partake of the same slippage it discovers.

I DON'T WANT TO KNOW ABOUT IT.

LANGUAGE IS SLIPPERY

It turns out that the very nature of language is such that its nearly infinite possibilities exceed the intentions of the speaker. The speaker in effect loses control over language. Part of this has to do with the fact that words are hardly ever <u>univocal</u> (having only one meaning). Look up in the dictionary an apparently straightforward word like "frog".

There is also the problem of metaphorical meaning which complicates the issue further. This is true whether the metaphor is used intentionally (as when Plato talks about "seeing" the ultimate Truth with the "mind's eye"), or is used unwittingly, as in the case of "dead metaphors" (this phrase itself is a "dead metaphor"), such as the references to the "legs" of a table, or the "face" of a clock — something of which Walt Disney's cartoons took great advantage (and now that Derrida teaches in Irvine, only a few miles from Disneyland, maybe, there's a connection between Disney's "theory" and Derrida's).

Metaphorical meaning cannot be kept out of literal meaning even if the speaker declares his or her intention of keeping it out. In philosophy and linguistics, metaphors have always been considered parasitic (another metaphor) on literal language. Derrida excels in demonstrating how they can dominate so-called literal meaning and transform it. (The opposition "literal/figurative" is another distinction Derrida "deconstructs".)

DISNEYLAND

LINES FOR
RIDES
FORM HERE

So, once language enters the public domain, the speaker or writer loses control of it, as it is always open to new understandings or misunderstandings.

This is because there is a fundamental UNDECIDABILITY built into language. Derrida's "deconstruction" reveals all the implications of this necessary instability in language.

Let us then finally try to say what **DECONSTRUCTION** is (a task made more difficult by Derrida's claim that it can't be defined). We have already seen that it is a way of reading texts such that all philosophical "first principles" (origins, absolutes) have been dismantled — or better, have been shown to dismantle themselves (like the hyena eating its own innards).

The same was true of the binary opposites on which so much of
human thought and discourse seems to depend. In one way,
this is just a radical continuation of the "critique of Reason"
begun by David Hume (1711-1776) and Immanuel Kant (1724-
1804), an attempt to think the limits of all possible thought.
The trouble is apparently one does not have to think back very
far to do this. Derrida seems to want to show that all texts
"come to embarrass their own ruling systems of logic," as one
commentator, Terry Eagleton, has put it, showing that all texts
display a surplus of meaning, and that the latent drift of textu-
al logic goes against its apparent intention. Deconstruction
locates the fissures, fault lines and stress points in texts where
rhetoric and authorial intention conflict. Often these vulnerable
spots are found in footnotes, margins, or parenthetical asides.
In fact, then, deconstruction is not just a method of analysis
or a way of reading texts. It is already at work within texts.

Well, then, what about Derrida's texts? Can they be decon-
structed too? Derrida does not seem to doubt it.
Deconstruction must be complicitous in the very discourse it
denounces. No form of human discourse can step outside of
discourse to render an antiseptic judgment about it.

In some ways, all this seems to be rather disastrous news, (or <u>liberating</u> news, depending on your perspective), because if Derrida, Barthes and Lacan are right, our only access to reality is a semiological one — that is, once language has been acquired, we are in contact with <u>signs</u>, not things. Derrida has gone so far as to say:

FROM THE MOMENT THAT THERE IS MEANING THERE ARE NOTHING BUT SIGNS. WE THINK ONLY IN SIGNS.

. . . and

IL N'Y A PAS DE HORS-TEXTE

HEY! LIVE IN ORANGE COUNTY, SPEAK ENGLISH!

[Oh, sorry!] THERE IS NOTHING OUTSIDE OF THE TEXT

(Some of Derrida's most ardent supporters, and Derrida himself, have since made efforts to diffuse this last, notorious statement.)

141

But perhaps this can only be accomplished with a kind of "kettle-logic" of the type related by Freud when he tells a joke about a man who confronts his neighbor over the fact that the kettle he had lent his neighbor was returned with a dent in it:

Here is some of the worst of the post-structuralist news: if language is constitutionally unstable, and if language creates the self, then the self is constitutionally unstable.

GLOSSARY

ALIENATION. A term from the philosophies of G.W.F Hegel and Karl Marx designating the loss of one's essence* as it is displaced* onto an alien object and confronts one as a form of otherness. (As, for example, when one understands one's being in terms of one's wealth and therefore fetishizes money.)

ARCHE-WRITING. A term coined by Jacques Derrida to designate the significant features that writing and speaking have in common such that the purported essential difference between the written word and the spoken word is demonstrated to be non-existent.

ATOMISM. Any theory that views reality as composed of discrete, irreducible units ("atoms" — from the Greek a-tomoi, "indivisible"), where the basic units are more real than the objects or events built up out of them. (Contrasts with ORGANI-CISM.*)

AVUNCULATE, THE. A supposed problem in anthropology concerning the relation of the maternal uncle to his nephew, a relation which is often either formal and authoritarian or informal and of a joking nature.

CONDENSATION. As used here, a term from Freudian psychoanalysis* designating a mode of primarily unconscious thought or mode of emotion in which two different images, meanings or emotions are collapsed into one. (Related to METAPHOR*)

DECONSTRUCTION. A term coined by Jacques Derrida naming the processes within language that produce a fundamental undecidability of meaning, one which often undermines the intention of the speaker or writer. Also the name of the method of reading texts which reveals that undecidability.

DETERMINISM. The metaphysical* view that necessity rules and that freedom is an illusion.

DIACHRONIC. Any analysis is diachronic if it concentrates on the historical development of the object of analysis. (Contrast with SYNCHRONIC*.)

DIALECTIC, THE. A term in the social theory of Karl Marx, borrowed from the philosophy of G.W.F. Hegel and modified to designate the fact that history progresses by resolving the contradictions between the opposing forces that make up any historical period (theses and antitheses) through revolutionary action (a synthesis). Also, in both Hegel and Marx, a scientific methodology in which socio-historical facts are analyzed in terms of relationships of opposition to and dependency upon each other.

DIFFÉRANCE. Jacques Derrida's neologism, pronounced the same way as the French word "différence" ("difference"), but intentionally misspelled. Designates the dual fact that (a) meaning is derived from difference, not sameness, and (b) meaning is never fully present but is always deferred, postponed.

DISPLACEMENT. As used here, a term from Freudian psychoanalysis* designating a mode of primarily unconscious thought or emotion in which the meaning or feeling about one image, word, or idea is transferred onto another one. (Related to METONYMY*.)

EGO, THE. In Freudian psychoanalysis*, the name of the rational, mostly conscious, social aspect of the psyche, as contrasted with the "id"* and the "superego"*.

EMPIRICISM. The theory according to which all knowledge derives from "experience," where "experience" is explicated in terms of sense-data.* Therefore, the view that all knowledge can be traced to direct observation.

ÉPISTÈME. A term coined by Michel Foucault derived from the Greek word for "knowledge," designating the whole of the system that organizes information and authorizes dispensation and control of "knowledge" during different historical periods.

ESSENCE. That characteristic (or set of characteristics) that an object has in common with similar objects and which allows members of the class of objects to be defined.

ESSENTIALISM. The metaphysical* view that in reality there exists not only individual objects, but also essences*.

EXISTENTIALISM. The term coined by Jean-Paul Sartre to name a philosophical position derived particularly from the nineteenth-century philosophers S. Kierkegaard and F. Nietzsche, according to which "existence precedes essence" This view entails the assertion that there is no such thing as "human nature," if that phrase is meant to designate characteristics that determine our behavior. Rather, the determinant of our behavior is our freedom.

FUNCTIONALISM. An anthropological theory according to which apparently bizarre, mysterious or otherwise inexplicable social phenomena are revealed to have some utilitarian value that tends to promote the survival of the culture.

HEDONISM. The philosophy which claims that pleasure is the highest value.

ID, THE. In Freudian psychoanalysis*, the name given to the mostly unconscious, anti-social, "animal" self, containing the primitive sexual and aggressive drives.

IDEOLOGY. A term from the philosophy of Karl Marx, naming a kind of (usually unconscious) political propaganda that is presented as fact while at the same time masking contradictions within the political system that it touts.

IMAGINARY, THE. A term from Lacanian psychoanalysis* designating not merely imagination or fantasy, but roughly everyday experience in all its naiveté, where the effects of the unconscious are not recognized, nor is the arbitrariness of the symbolic*.

INNATE IDEA. An idea present at birth, hence not derived from experience. Rationalism* based its theory of knowledge on the foundational nature of such inborn concepts.

LANGUE, LA. A term in Saussurean linguistics designating the synchronic* state of the whole set of phonic and conventional relations (grammar, syntax, semantics) that constitute a language. (Contrast with LA PAROLE*.)

LOGOCENTRISM. A term coined by Jacques Derrida to name what he takes to be the dominant metaphysics* of the West, a metaphysics prioritizing the spoken word (equated with Spirit, fullness, presence, and immediate Truth) over the written word (equated with mere imitation of the Truth, or supplement to it and falsification of it). It is Derrida's intention to submit logocentrism to the process of "deconstruction."*

METAPHOR. The combination of two apparently unrelated images or ideas to form a new figure of speech involving meaning through comparison. E.g., "George Washington is the Father of our Country;" "Jesus is the lamb of God."

METAPHYSICS. As used here, a complete philosophical view of the totality of reality, encompassing a theory of reality, of ethics, aesthetics and logic, and how all these fields relate to one another. (See also: Weltanschauung*.)

METONYMY. A figure of speech in which an object is named by using the part for the whole (e.g., "the Crowns of Europe"), or by using something tangentially assoicated with the object to name the object (e.g., "Joe likes the bottle too much").

MIRROR STAGE, THE. A term from Lacanian psychoanalysis* designating a moment of infantile development between 6 and 18 months when the infant recognizes its own image as being both itself and not itself. The ability to enter fully into a linguistic community is dependent upon this stage.

MYTHEMES. A term from the structural anthropology of Claude Lévi-Strauss designating what he takes to be the basic units of meaning in myths (e.g., hot, cold, sweet, sour, etc.) derived by analogy from the idea of a "phoneme" (basic unit of sound) in linguistics.

OEDIPUS COMPLEX, THE. A term in Freudian psychoanalysis* designating an ontogenetic* and a phylogenetic* propensity for the child to be erotically attracted to the parent of the opposite sex, and to experience a state of jealous competition with the parent of the same sex. De-biologized and transformed by Jacques Lacan into "the Oedipus," designating the subject's entry into the Symbolic* under the dominion of "The Law of the Father."

ONOMATOPOEIA. Words that sound like the noise or object they name, such as "buzz," "burp," "hum," "bark."

ONTOGENY. Developmental analysis of the history of an individual. (Contrast with PHYLOGENY.*)

ORGANICISM. Any theory that views reality as being like an organism, wherein the parts are real only insofar as they are related to each other and to the totality. (Contrast with ATOMISM*.)

PARADIGMATIC. As used here, a term in linguistics designating the "vertical" feature of language whereby one term in a sentence can be meaningfully replaced by a related term. E.g., "dog" for "animal," and "terrier" for "dog" in the sentence, "The animal jumped over the fence." (Contrast with SYNTAGMATIC*.)

PAROLE, LA. A term in Saussurean linguistics designating the individual speech-acts that activate features of la langue* to create communicative events.

PHENOMENOLOGY. Literally, "the study of appearances," but in the philosophy of Edmund Husserl (1859-1938), a method of analyzing the structure and content of consciousness.

PHYLOGENY. Developmental analysis of a biologically related group: a phylum, a species, a sub-species. (Contrast with ONTOGENY*.)

POSITIVISM. As used here, the worship of science, and the view that all truths can ultimately be stated in terms of scientific laws.

POST-STRUCTURALISM. The name of a loosely-knit intellectual movement that emerged out of structuralism* after some of the practitioners of that theory either became dissatisfied with the strictures and confinements of Saussurean linguistics (upon which structuralism was based) or claimed to discover features of those linguistics which, when carried to their logical extremes, were self-defeating and undermined structuralism itself. In post-structuralism, language, meaning, social institutions and the self are destabilized.

PRIMORDIAL PATRICIDE, THE. A term from Freudian psychoanalysis* designating the supposed murder of an aboriginal father by his sons, a murder producing unconscious guilt in the primal sons which becomes the foundation of the social and psychological institutions of historical culture.

PSYCHOANALYSIS. the name of the theory of Sigmund Freud (1856-1939) that studies individuals and cultures by explaining mental and social phenomena in terms of the dynamics between the unconscious and the conscious mind. Also the name of the psychotherapy based on that theory.

RATIONALISM. the metaphysical* view that (a) everything in reality is logically consistent with everything else in reality, and the view that (b) this logical consistency can be grasped by the human mind, because (c) the human mind reflects the logical structure of reality.

REAL, THE. A term from Lacanian psychoanalysis* provoking much debate among interpreters. "The Real" is "in place" and all forms of representation (images, pictures, symbols, words) are "out of place," necessarily deflected from "the Real," which is that in experience which resists all representation. It is the experiential residue that can be approached but never possessed after entrance into the Imaginary* and the Symbolic*.

REALISM. The metaphysical* view that there is an objective reality to which human subjectivity has access.

RELATIVISM. The denial of absolute truths or absolute facts, and the claim that the truths and facts achieve their "truthfulness" or "factualness" only relative to other "truths" or "facts" which are themselves relative to yet other "truths" or "facts."

SEMIOLOGY. The study of "signs,"* encompassing linguistics, but also dealing with other systems of signs, such as gestures, dress codes and rules of conduct.

SENSE-DATA. A sense-datum is that which is perceived immediately by any one of the senses prior to interpretation by the mind. (E.g., colors, sounds, tastes, odors, tactile sensations, pleasures and pains.)

SIGN. As used here, a term from Saussurean linguistics designating the unit of meaning composed of the combination of a "signifier"* and a "signified."*

DREAMS AND MADNESS, THEN, APPEARED TO BE OF THE SAME SUBSTANCE.

SIGNIFIED. In Saussurean linguistics, the idea or concept designated by a "signifier"* and combining with it to create a "sign." (E.g., the idea of the family, <u>Felidae</u>, designated by the signifier, "kat" combining to form the sign, "cat.")

SIGNIFIER. In Saussurean linguistics, the audio-image (sound) or visual image that is associated by convention with a "signified"* to create a "sign."* (E.g., the sound "d—g" designating the signified, the family, <u>Canis Familiaris</u>, combining to form the sign, "dog.")

SOLIPSISM. The metaphysical* view that "<u>My</u> world is <u>the</u> world," or, more technically, that one only has access to the contents of one's own mind, hence one has no good reason to believe in the existence of anything other than one's own mind.

STRUCTURALISM. The theory of social reality that applies the principles of the science of linguistics to all social phenomena, such that social meaning is reducible to a system of oppositional relationships ("structures") which define "sameness" and "otherness."

SUBLATION. A term from the Hegelian dialectic* representing the moment of synthesis between opposing historical contradictions (viz., theses and antitheses) such that this synthesis is an overcoming of these contradictions and a transcending of the historical conditions creating conflict.

SUPEREGO, THE. In Freudian psychoanalysis* the name given to that component of the psyche that counteracts anti-social impulses of the id* by producing conscious and unconscious feelings of guilt.

SUPERSTRUCTURE, THE. A term from the philosophy of Karl Marx designating all those aspects of society (viz., law, politics, religion, philosophy, literature, art) that are built up upon and reflect at a distance the nature of the economic foundation of society and the interests of the class that controls that foundation.

SYMBOLIC, THE. A term from Lacanian psychoanalysis* designating not only the realm of language and law, but also of all aspects of representation: signs*, symbols, meanings. The realm that imposes order on experience and the realm in which the subject is determined.

SYNCHRONIC. Any analysis is "synchronic" if it concentrates exclusively on the current state of the object under investigation, describing all of its present features and relationships at the expense of their historical development. (Contrast with DIACHRONIC.*)

SYNTAGMATIC. A term in linguistics designating that "horizontal" feature of language whereby a sequence of parts of speech can be developed into meaningful phrases. E.g., the sequence: subject - conjugated verb - object that allows the sentences, "Mary sues her lawyer," and "Sue marries her lawyer" to be meaningful. (Contrast with PARADIGMATIC.*)

SYNTHETIC A PRIORI. A term from the philosophy of Immanuel Kant (1724-1804) supposedly designating a kind of <u>meaningful truth about reality</u> (="synthetic") <u>known to be true independent of observation</u> (=a priori). Kant believed this category included propositions like: "space is real," "time is real," "every event is caused," as well as the whole of mathematics.

TOTEMISM. The social organization shared by many "primitive" societies according to which each member of the social unit traces ancestry to a supernatural animal, the "totem."

WELTANSCHAUUNG. German for "world-view." An overall picture of reality in which all of its parts are seen as being interrelated. (See also METAPHYSICS*.)

BIBLIOGRAPHY

I. GENERAL WORKS ON STRUCTURALISM AND POSTSTRUCTURALISM.

DeGeorge, Richard and Fernande, eds. <u>The Structuralists From Marx to Lévi-Strauss,</u> Garden City, N.Y.: Doubleday Anchor Books, 1972.

Eagleton, Terry, <u>Literary Theory: An Introduction,</u> Minneapolis: University of Minnesota Press, 1983.

Hawkes, Terence, <u>Structuralism and Semiotics,</u> Berkeley: University of California Press, 1977.

Lechte, John, <u>Fifty Key Contemporary Thinkers: From Structuralism to Postmodernity</u>, London and New York, Routledge, 1994.

Megill, Allan, <u>Prophets Of Extremity: Nietzche, Heidegger, Foucault and Derrida</u>, Berkely: University of California Press, 1985.

Sturrock, John, ed., <u>Structuralism and Since: From Lévi-Strauss to Derrida,</u> Oxford and New York: Oxford University Press, 1979.

II. FERDINAND DE SAUSSURE

A. MAIN WORK AVAILABLE IN ENGLISH.

<u>Course in General Linguistics,</u> trans. Wade Baskin, New York: Philosophical Library, 1959. Or...

<u>Course in General Linguistics,</u> trans. Roy Harris, Lasalle, Illinois: Open Court, 1994.

B. BOOKS ABOUT SAUSSURE.

Culler, Jonathan, <u>Ferdinand de Saussure,</u> Ithica, New York: Cornell University Press, 1986.

Gordon, W. Terrence, <u>Saussure for Beginners,</u> New York: Writers and Readers, 1996.

III. CLAUDE LEVI-STRAUSS

A. MAIN WORKS AVAILABLE IN ENGLISH.

Introduction to a Science of Mythology
Volume I: <u>The Raw and the Cooked,</u> trans. John and Doreen Weightman, London: Jonathan Cape, 1978

Volume II: <u>From Honey to Ashes,</u> trans. John and Doreen Weightman, London: Jonathan Cape, 1973.

<u>**Volume IV: The Naked Man,**</u> **trans. John and Doreen Weightman, London:** Jonathan Cape, 1981.

<u>The Jealous Potter,</u> trans. Bénédicte Chorier, Chicago: University of Chicago Press, 1988.

<u>The Savage Mind</u>, trans. George Weiderfeld and Nicolson Ltd., Chicago: University of Chicago Press, 1966.

<u>Structural Anthropology</u>, trans. Claire Jacobsen and Brooke Grundfest Schoepf, New York: Basic Books, 1963.

<u>Totemism Today,</u> trans. Rodney needham, Boston: Beacon Press, 1963.

<u>Tristes Tropiques,</u> trans. John Russell, New York: Atheneum, 1964.

B. BOOKS ABOUT LÉVI-STRAUSS.

Pace, David, <u>Claude Lévi-Strauss, the Bearer of Ashes,</u>
    Boston: Routledge & Kegan Paul, 1983.
Leach, Edmund, <u>Lévi-Strauss,</u> London: Fontana/Collins,
    1970.

IV. ROLAND BARTHES.

A. MAIN WORKS AVAILABLE IN ENGLISH.

<u>A Lover's Discourse: Fragments,</u> trans. Richard Howard,
    New York: Hill and Wang, 1978.
<u>Elements of Semiology,</u> trans. Annette Lavers and Colin Smith,
    New York: Hill and Wang, 1968.
<u>Empire of Signs,</u> trans. Richard Howard, Evanston: Northwestern
    University Press, 1972.
<u>Image-Music-Text,</u> trans. Stephen Heath, New York: Hill and Wang, 1977.
<u>Mythologies,</u> trans. Annette Lavers, New York: Hill and Wang, 1983.
<u>On Racine,</u> trans. Richard Howard, New York: Hill and Wang, 1964.
<u>The Pleasure of the Text,</u> trans. Richard Miller, New York: Hill and Wang, 1975.
<u>Roland Barthes by Roland Barthes,</u> trans. Richard Howard, New York: Hill and Wang, 1977.
<u>S/Z,</u> trans. Richard Miller, New York: Hill and Wang, 1977.
<u>Writing Zero Degree,</u> trans. Annette Lavers and Colin Smith, New York: Hill and Wang,
    1968.

B. BOOK ABOUT BARTHES.

Culler, Jonathan, <u>Barthes,</u> New York: Oxford University Press, 1983.

IV. JACQUES LACAN.

A. MAIN WORKS BY LACAN AVAILABLE IN ENGLISH.

<u>Ecrits: A Selection,</u> trans. Alan Sheridan, New York: W.W. Norton, 1982.
<u>The Four Fundamental Concepts of Psycho-Analysis,</u> trans. Alan Sheridan, New York: W.W.
    Norton, 1978.
<u>The Language of the Self,</u> ed. and trans. Anthony Wilden, Baltimore: Johns Hopkins
    University Press, 1968.

B. BOOKS ABOUT LACAN.

Hill, Phillip, <u>Lacan for Beginners,</u> New York: Writers and Readers, 1997.
Lemaire, Anika, <u>Jacques Lacan,</u> trans. David Macey, Boston: Routledge & Kegan Paul, 1977.
MacCannell, Juliette, <u>Figuring Lacan: Criticism and the Cultural Unconscious,</u> London: Croom
    Helm, 1986.

VI. MICHEL FOUCAULT.

A. MAIN WORKS BY FOUCAULT AVAILABLE IN ENGLISH.

<u>The Archaeology of Knowledge and Discourse on Language,</u> trans. A.M. Sheridan- Smith,
    New York: Pantheon, 1972.
<u>The Birth of the Clinic: An Archaeology of Medical Perception,</u> trans. A.M. Sheridan-Smith,
    New York: Random House Vintage Books, 1975.

Discipline and Punish: The Birth of the Prison, trans. Alan Sheridan, New York: Random House Vintage Books, 1979.

The History of Sexuality:
> Volume I: An Introduction, trans. Robert Hurley, New York: Random House Vintage Books, 1980.
> Volume II: The Use of Pleasure, trans. Robert Hurley, New York: Pantheon, 1985.
> Volume III: The Care of the Self, trans. Robert Hurley, New York: Pantheon, 1986.

Madness and Civilization: A History of Insanity in the Age of Reason. trans. Richard Howard, New York: Random House Vintage Books, 1973.

The Order of Things: An Archaeology of the Human Sciences, trans.(none listed), New York: Random House Vintage Books, 1973.

Power/Knowledge: Selected Interview and Other Writings, 1972-1977, ed.Colin Gordon, trans. Colin Gordon, Leo Marshall, John Mephan, Kate Soper, New York: Pantheon, 1980.

B. BOOKS ABOUT FOUCAULT

Dreyfus, Hubert, and Rabinow, Paul, Michel Foucault: Beyond Structuralism and Hermeneutics, Chicago: University of Chicago Press, 1983.
Fillingham, Lydia Alix, Foucault for Beginners, New York: Writers and Readers, 1995.
Poster, Mark, Foucault, Marxism and History, London: Blackwell, 1984.

VII. JACQUES DERRIDA.

A. MAIN WORKS BY DERRIDA AVAILABLE IN ENGLISH.

Dissemination, trans. Barbara Johnson, London: Athlone Press: 1981.
Margins of Philosophy, trans. Alan Bassm Chicago: University of Chicago Press, 1982.
Of Grammatology, trans. Gayatri Chakravorty Spivak, Baltimore: Johns Hopkins University Press, 1976.
Positions, trans. Alan Bass, Chicago: University of Chicago Press, 1981.
Spurs: Nietzsche's Styles, trans. Barbara Harlow, Chicago: University of Chicago Press, 1979.
Writing and Difference, trans. Alan Bass, London: Routledge & Kegan Paul, 1978.

BOOKS ABOUT DERRIDA.

Norris, Christopher, Derrida, Cambridge: Harvard University Press, 1987.
Powell, James, Derrida for Beginners, New York: Writers and Readers, 1997.

QUOTE CITATIONS

Key:

AK = Michel Foucault, <u>The Archaeology of Knowledge,</u> trans. A.M. Sheridan-Smith, New York: Pantheon, 1972.

BB = Roland Barthes, <u>Roland Barthes by Roland Barthes,</u> trans. Richard Howard, New York: Hill and Wang, 1977.

É = Jacques Lacan, <u>Écrits: A Selection,</u> trans. Alan Sheridan, New York: W.W. Norton, 1982.

GL = Ferdinand de Saussure, <u>Course in General Linguistics,</u> trans. Wade Baskin, New York Philosophical Library, 1959.

IMT = Roland Barthes, <u>Image-Music-Text,</u> trans. Stephen Heath, New York: Hill and Wang, 1997.

MC = Michel Foucault, <u>Madness and Civilization,</u> trans. Richard Howard, New York: Random House Vintage, 1973.

MY= Roland Barthes, <u>Mythologies,</u> trans. Annette Lavers, New York: Hill and Wang, 1983.

OG = Jacques Derrida, <u>Of Grammatology,</u> trans. Gayatri Chakravorty Spivak, Baltimore: Johns Hopkins University Press, 1976.

P/K= <u>Power/Knowledge,</u> ed. Colin Gordon, trans. Colin Gordon, Leo Marshall, John Mepham, Kate Soper, New York: Pantheon, 1980.

PO = Jacques Derrida, <u>Positions,</u> trans. Alan Bass, Chicago: University of Chicago Press, 1981.

SA = Claude Lévi-Strauss, <u>Structural Anthropology,</u> trans. Claire Jacobsen and Brooke Grundfest Schoepf, New York: Basic Books, 1963.

SM = Claude Lévi-Strauss, <u>The Savage Mind,</u> trans. George Weiderfeld and Nicolson Ltd., Chicago: University of Chicago Press, 1966.

TT = Claude Lévi-Strauss, <u>Totemism Today,</u> trans. Rodney Needham, Boston: Beacon Press, 1963.

The left column designates page numbers from <u>Structuralism and Post-structuralism for Beginners.</u> The right column designates page numbers from the works keyed above. First and last words from each quotation are listed.

INDEX

Donald Palmer is Emeritus Professor of Philosophy at the college of Marin in Kentfield, California. Currently he is visiting Assistant Professor of Philosophy at North carolina State University in Raleigh, North Carolina. He is also author of:
Sartre For Beginners, Writers and Readers Publishing, Inc.
Kierkegaard For Beginners, Writers and Readers Publishing, Inc.
Looking at Philosophy, Mayfield Publishing Co.
Does the Center Hold?, Mayfield Publishing Co.